8 Things

We Hate

About I.T.

How to Move Beyond
the Frustrations
to Form a New
Partnership with I.T.

Susan Cramm

HARVARD BUSINESS PRESS
BOSTON, MASSACHUSETTS

Library of Congress Cataloging-in-Publication Data

Cramm, Susan.

8 things we hate about IT : how to move beyond the frustrations to form a new partnership with IT / Susan Cramm.

   p. cm.

  ISBN 978-1-4221-3166-4 (hardcover : alk. paper)

  1. Information technology—Management.   2. Business enterprises—Computer networks.   3. Management information systems.   I. Title.   II. Title: Eight things we hate about IT.

  HD30.2.C718 2010

  004.068'4—dc22

2009040841

Three rules of work: Out of clutter find simplicity;
from discord find harmony; in the middle of
difficulty lies opportunity.

—Albert Einstein

CONTENTS

Introduction   1

1. You Need Service, and IT Needs Control   15

2. You Need Results, and IT Needs Respect   29

3. You Need to Focus on Tactics, and IT Needs
   Strategic Alignment   43

4. You Need IT Funding, and IT Needs Returns   63

5. You Need On-time Delivery, and IT Needs Quality   85

6. You Need Customization, and IT Needs
   Standardization   107

7. You Need Innovation, and IT Functions in
   Bureaucracy   125

8. You Need Good IT, and IT Can Become Great   141

APPENDIX A: *A Primer on Fast-Cycle Development*   157
APPENDIX B: *Emerging Technologies*   161
APPENDIX C: *Key Responsibilities of the
            New Business–IT Partnership*   167
Notes   171
Index   181
About the Author   193

Introduction

Getting what you want out of information technology is difficult—very difficult. *By the time it's delivered, it disappoints.* It's always too little, too late, for too much. *When we finally get new technology, we don't use it.* My HDTV has network connections that will remain forever disconnected. On average, Microsoft Word users master only about 5 percent of the available features, and the typical company exploits only a small fraction of the functionality available in its enterprise resource planning (ERP) software. *Once we have it, we want to replace it.* I've hated my laptop since the day I bought it. My husband's new iPhone is like a siren calling me, even though my BlackBerry arrived only a few months ago.

Old is OK for wine and furniture, but new technology, by definition, must be better—at least until we get it. Let's face it: we are commitment-phobic when it comes to IT.

For personal uses, troubled technology isn't a problem, it's an annoyance—something to complain about but not fix (did I mention that the DVD drive on my laptop has been broken for two months, even though it is still under warranty?). If we can't Ctrl-Alt-Delete the problem away, we can always go shopping. Smart phone freezing? Buy another one. Laptop slowing down? Buy an Apple. Hard disk crash? Subscribe to an online backup service. Sure, it's expensive, but we want the new stuff anyway. After all, it's bright and shiny and includes lots of whiz-bang features—some that we may actually use.

Businesses can't buy their way out of troubled technology. We are already spending too much of our precious capital on technology, losing billions on failed and troubled projects, and jeopardizing our top-line revenue because of systems degradation, downtime, and inadvertent leaks of our customers' private information. Our business processes are embedded in brittle and complex technology, and the future of our companies depends on transforming this mess into "digitized" capabilities that will allow us to rapidly innovate and propagate new products, services, and business models. A response to my blog perfectly articulated the challenge facing us: "Here's a scary thought—what if this is as good as it gets? My sense is that . . . complexity is going to keep growing faster than our ability to manage it."[1]

No doubt the current model is ripe for an overhaul. It's hard to remember the time when criticizing IT was controversial. The classic *Harvard Business Review* article "IT Doesn't Matter" resonated because it underscored the pervasive belief that IT mediocrity is the norm.[2] How bad is a profession's reputation when a major outsourcer can get away with insulting its target market with the slogan "We Do IT Right"? One of my readers shared his frustrations with IT and what he believes the role of the IT organization should be: "My biggest frustration with IT is . . . they stifle creative entrepreneurialism that is critical to advancing the state of the business . . . IT should not just carry out specific needs, it should creatively partner to explore what SHOULD be done."[3] *If you take a poll, you'll find that almost every IT professional across the globe agrees.* The problem is that the IT organization is so busy managing the trees, it can't think about the forest. IT leaders spend the vast majority of their time grappling with lights-on activities and the remainder fielding enhancement and project requests that overwhelm available resources.

Eventually, we will learn how to manage technology rather than let technology manage us. In ten or twenty years, we will be well on our way to having Lego-like technology, available on a pay-per-use basis, that connects anyone and anything, anytime, anywhere. These Lego blocks will be in the hands of IT-smart, business-leader digital natives (versus digital nomads), allowing them to fulfill their day-to-day IT needs on their own. When this all comes together, the IT organization will finally be positioned to enable rather than inhibit change.

Until this glorious day arrives, you have a job to do. And that's what this book is about—helping you get what you want out of technology by moving beyond frustrations and forming a new partnership with IT.

Blame the System, Not the People

When it comes to IT, business leaders feel like strangers in a strange land. Getting projects approved and funded means attending a dizzying array of meetings and seemingly endless working and reworking of business cases. Starting projects requires a breadth of specialists that rivals the holiday party list at the Mayo Clinic. Defining functionality and detailed design heralds a litany of requirements and architectural documents that require multiple levels of business and IT approvals. Developing the solutions entails not only programming but also endless change requests, tests, documentation, and training classes.

At turnover, project teams disband and your new technology is thrust into the cold arms of operations, where communications are routed through a call center and documented in incident reports that must be escalated before resolution. You know that, deep in the bowels of a server somewhere, your system is running, a sequence of zeroes and 1's zipping through integrated circuits, miraculously delivering critical information to your sales force when they need it, wherever they are. But the accomplishment feels hollow in light of the painful process, the mountain of paperwork, and the fact that the project blew by the estimated budget and timeline by a significant factor.

It's overwhelming and more than a little scary. Technology is a key to your success, but you don't have a clue about how to manage it. It's tempting, but not productive, to blame the IT organization. IT delivers complex services to relatively unsophisticated and demanding customers who expect IT to serve their individual interests without regard to the benefit and risks to the enterprise. Much of what frustrates business leaders about the IT organization is their inability to exert more control over the IT assets that fuel the business and navigate the bureaucracy that has been put in place to ensure that the whole of IT is greater than the sum of its parts.

When frustrated, we all tend to blame others. It's difficult to see the larger context and easier to cast negative attributions and form mental models that explain our perceptions and justify our feelings. Check out table I-1, which lists the negative mental models that keep business and IT leaders from developing productive, positive, mutually satisfying relationships.[4]

None of the mental models is right, but neither are they wrong. The key to reconciling them is to shift your perspective, look through the eyes of your partners in IT, and understand the context in which they operate. Doing so will allow you to develop a single version of the truth and will give you the insight necessary to change the relationship for the better. No rational

TABLE I-1

The 8 hates

	Line leaders hate when IT . . .	IT leaders hate when the business . . .
Service or control	Is overly bureaucratic and control oriented	Makes half-baked requests and is clueless about impact
Results or respect	Consists of condescending techies who don't listen	Treats IT professionals like untrustworthy servant-genies
Tactics or strategy	Is reactive rather than proactive	Develops plans without including IT
Expense or investment	Proposes "deluxe" when "good enough" will do	Focuses on costs and not value
Quickness or quality	Doesn't deliver on time	Changes its mind all the time
Customization or standardization	Doesn't understand the true needs of the business	Wants it all—right now—regardless of ROI
Innovation or bureaucracy	Doesn't support innovation	Isn't IT-smart and doesn't use or understand IT systems
Greatness or goodness	Inhibits business change	Is never satisfied with IT

person hates the people in IT (or the business), but everybody—IT and business leaders alike—hates the current IT system. Even IT's powers that be are frustrated. Case in point, a *Fortune Global 200* CIO described IT to me as a "sucking vortex."

There is no way out. Business leaders need to become smarter about how to lead with technology and how to work with IT. Fortunately, the gain is worth the pain. Companies that are smart about managing IT outperform those that aren't. Under-performing companies make bad investments, ignore the inherent risks of developing and deploying technology, and spend too much time and money operating fragmented systems using informal, undocumented processes. For these underperformers, there is no correlation between IT spending and financial outcomes. To paraphrase Peter Weill and Jeanne Ross in their book *IT Savvy,* if you don't figure out how to make IT a strategic asset, it will become a strategic liability.[5]

Becoming IT-Smart

IT-smart business leaders are masters at navigating the IT organizational bureaucracy, cutting through the jargon, managing IT-enabled change, demonstrating tangible business value, leveraging the technology on the shelves, and fostering innovation within their teams.

Unfortunately, in a recent survey, only 27 percent of business leaders are considered IT-smart (i.e., earned a grade of *A* or *B* from IT and business leaders on how well they leverage technology). The good news is that companies with IT-smart business leaders report more productive IT-business relationships and fewer frustrations (see table I-2) than those with IT-dumb business leaders (who earned a grade of *D* or *F*).[6]

TABLE I-2

Implications of IT-smart business leaders

How IT-smart are our organizations?	IT-dumb	IT-smart
Technology is considered a competitive weapon or is starting to provide differentiation.	26%[a]	56%
Technology investments have provided great or acceptable ROI.	31%	85%
Business leaders are accountable for realizing value or take the lead in justifying IT-enabled initiatives.	16%	53%
Business leaders drive IT-enabled change.	39%	72%
Business and IT leaders identify IT needs collaboratively when developing business strategy.	10%	48%
The business makes half-baked requests and is clueless about enterprise impact.	78%	35%
IT doesn't deliver on time.	50%	35%
IT consists of technologists, not business leaders.	62%	33%
The business always changes its mind about what it want its systems to do.	74%	40%
The business doesn't know how to use its systems.	79%	25%

a. Numbers reflect the percentage of respondents who agree or strongly agree with statements.

Knowing more about technology and the supporting processes will make your dealings with IT more efficient. A good grasp of IT terminology and key processes (to get new technology funded and delivered and existing technology up and operational) will help ensure that your people and processes have the information and tools they need.

Even more powerful, creating strong relationships with the people in IT will make you more effective in getting what you want out of IT (besides making the time spent huddled together in conference rooms a lot more enjoyable). With a little help from your friends, you can make the system work for you, and not against you.

From Good to Great

If you are an overachiever, it's likely that when you looked at the survey results you noticed that improving IT smarts gets us from "bad" to "good" but to not to "great." To position IT as a competitive advantage, companies need to democratize IT-enabled innovation. Business leaders and their teams need to spend less time waiting for IT resources and more time innovating.

For its part, IT needs to spend less time trying to figure out how to satisfy a hundred pounds of demand with twenty-five pounds of supply and more time creating tools that allow their business counterparts to innovate and satisfy their day-to-day needs on their own. Getting to great IT, discussed further in chapter 8, is a ten- to twenty-year journey that is impossible without IT-smart business leaders. This book is focused on helping business leaders become smarter about IT so that they can help bring this future forward.

Why I Wrote This Book

I have been involved with IT throughout most of my thirty-year career, starting as a programmer, then a CIO and a CFO, and, since 1998, a leadership coach helping executives make sense out of technology. I did have a moment of weakness and left my CIO role to be a CFO for four years. The job was easier but, alas, not nearly as interesting, and I found myself back in IT, nagging leaders to get it right. But I'm feeling restless again, understanding that IT's impact is limited unless business leaders learn how to lead with technology.

So I shifted the focus of my writing from IT leaders to business leaders, with the goal of helping business leaders manage the technology that fuels their business. In early 2008, I started writing a blog, Have IT Your Way, for Harvard Business Online, and one of the first pieces I wrote was titled "The Eight Things We Hate About IT." I had no idea that the outpouring of responses would be so emotional, and I quickly learned that there were a lot of frustrations but not a lot of insights—by business or IT leaders—about how to channel the emotion toward a productive end.

This book is written for leaders who make the business rock 'n' roll on a daily basis but don't control enterprise-level decisions regarding strategy, annual goals and objectives, financial and head count allocations, and the like. As someone taught me many, many years ago, businesses aren't run by CXO-level executives but by the people on the front lines working with customers or supporting the people who do. These operational leaders are the people who work with IT on a day-in, day-out basis, and if this book helps improve the quality of their interactions with the IT organization and the impact from their IT-enabled investments, then I can sleep soundly knowing it has helped businesses manage IT as an organizational asset and not simply as an organizational structure.

There are plenty of books and articles to help CXO- and board-level executives improve how they leverage and govern IT. That's a good thing, given that senior executives "frequently lack the fundamental knowledge needed to ask intelligent questions about IT in terms of risks and costs."[7] But even if you have knowledge at the top, it's not enough. IT leadership needs to be a core competence throughout the organization so that senior-level direction is executed effectively and frontline innovation occurs as a natural course of business.

In writing this book, I had the overarching goal to communicate IT leadership principles in a robust but simple manner—attempting, in the words of Albert Einstein, to "make everything as simple as possible, but not simpler."[8] Everyone knows that IT is complex, but not enough people understand that within the complexity are simple, timeless truths that, if respected, will help leaders manage the complexity. Toward that end, this book is as jargon free as possible, with plenty of footnotes providing more information and references for those who want to learn more.

How to Use This Book

If you are a business leader and experienced in managing technology, this book will be helpful in educating your team and improving their relationship with IT. If you aren't experienced in managing technology, this book will help you grasp the fundamental principles and determine what you should demand of yourself and your team and what you should expect from the IT organization.

As you implement these principles, consider them absolutes. Don't let your team or your counterparts in IT convince you that your situation is unique and can't be approached as recommended. For example, when developing new IT-enabled capabilities, most agree that implementing increments of change and value every three to six months is less risky and more successful than implementing all at once, two or three years out. But faced with reality, people often rationalize that the iterative approach doesn't apply (for example, due to the complexity of existing processes, the time it takes to obtain funding, the rework required to ensure that the increments fit together, etc.). Don't fall into this trap. The principle is about delivering value, not just technology, every three to six months, using any creative combination of people, process, and technology you can think of to build organizational support and transform the capabilities of your organization.

Of course, once you have mastered these principles and have a track record of success in managing IT, you can apply them with more creativity and nuance, taking measured risks, and achieve even more powerful results.

If you are an IT leader, this book will be useful in educating your team about IT–business collaboration and in engaging business partners in creating a more satisfying and productive relationship. Many IT professionals have spent their entire career in IT, and this book will help them shift perspectives and look at their world from the point of view of their business partners. You may bristle at some of these leadership principles, viewing them as too black-and-white. Instead of dismissing them, use them to stimulate discussion within your team and with business partners about what is going well, what isn't, and how the principles can be applied to further progress.

What to Expect in This Book

This book is organized by the "eight hates" outlined earlier, with a chapter dedicated to each where I examine and reconcile the frustrations. My goal is to help you change the *ors* in table I-1 into *ands* by answering the following questions:

- **Chapter 1:** How can we serve the needs of the business in a controlled manner?

- **Chapter 2:** How can we deliver results while enhancing relationships?

- **Chapter 3:** How can we identify tactics that are grounded in strategy?

- **Chapter 4:** How can we make sure our expenses are investments?

- **Chapter 5:** How can deliver quickly, with quality?

- **Chapter 6:** How can we have customized standardization?

- **Chapter 7:** How can we innovate in spite of the bureaucracy?

- **Chapter 8:** How can we transform IT from good to great?

In reading this book, business leaders may feel that IT leaders are being let off the hook, making the whole IT–business relationship the business leaders' problem to solve. If you are to serve as a catalyst for positive change, this is the only productive point of view. The only person you can change is yourself, and, in the process of changing yourself, your counterparts in IT will be forced to change. Great relationships aren't 50-50, they're 100-100, with each party doing whatever it can to meet the needs of the other. But rest assured, although most of the book is focused on nagging you, the business leader, the end of each chapter holds your IT counterparts accountable by summarizing what you should expect from them. In addition, chapter 8 outlines how to serve yourself if you find that, in spite of all your valiant efforts, IT is incapable of doing so.

Who You Can Blame

This book is my baby. If you like it, please adopt it. If you don't, I hope that it makes you think and develop your own point of view about how to better manage technology and work with the IT organization. If you decide to disregard the book, please don't disregard all the wonderful work included in the references. There are a lot of brilliant practitioners, academics, service providers, and research organizations working hard trying to crack this intractable nut. Don't throw their bathwater out with this baby. Finally, I would love to hear your perspectives, so please feel free to e-mail me at susan@valuedance.com.

Who I Want to Thank

Thanks to Paul Michelman, from Harvard Business Press, who saw something that I could barely see myself and encouraged me to write this book. Thanks as well to my editor, Kathleen Carr, who has a light, right hand, and the team members at Harvard Business School Publishing, who are a pleasure to work with in every way. Also thanks to my clients, who continue to inspire, educate, and support me, and the companies who employed me and allowed me to learn on their nickel.

Of course, in the grand "Why are we here?" scheme of things, this book doesn't really matter. What does matter are the hands you hold and those you care for. Writing a book, or committing one's time to any intense endeavor, is ultimately a selfish act. I now know why authors always thank/apologize to their spouses and family. I, too, must thank and apologize to my dear husband, Bryan, and fun sidekick, Jessica. In his gentle, supportive, funny way, Bryan taught me that living in my head isn't nearly as fun as living in the world.

1

You Need Service, and IT Needs Control

Your IT leaders want nothing more than to make their business counterparts happy.

Why wouldn't they? You are line; they are staff. You hang out with the external customers and drive the top line; they hang out in buildings down the street and drive (up) the middle of the P&L. You may not hire them, but you can get them fired; many an IT leader has had to pack his bags, having failed to understand how to play well with his business counterparts. On a day-in, day-out basis, you call the shots. You're the man.

IT leaders not only want to please you because you pay their mortgage, but also they're excited about helping solve big, chunky problems. Most IT folks get into the profession because they love solving puzzles and want a chance to sort out a mess and find a better way.[1]

Unfortunately, you aren't the *only* man. IT has two major stakeholders: you (actually, many, many of you) and the enterprise. Business leaders spend most of their time on the here and now, figuring out how to organize their scarce resources to sell and deliver products to picky customers who want more for less. In contrast, the enterprise needs to balance the near term with the long term. That's why even though IT leaders want to say yes, they usually don't have the authority to do so (see table 1-1).

In IT-smart companies with streetwise CIOs, the responsibility for saying "Yes, but . . ." is shifted from IT and placed on the broader shoulders of enterprise IT governance boards, which make decisions about strategy, funding, projects, architecture, and risk.[2] This arrangement relieves IT of its control responsibilities and frees it to focus first and foremost on serving business leaders.

Unfortunately, a lot of IT-dumb companies have business leaders who don't understand why IT insists on setting up seemingly bureaucratic oversight that operates as a puppet regime of the CIO. Business leaders resent having to jump through hoops so that their requests can be reviewed by CXOs who aren't all that comfortable with or interested in making IT-related decisions, only to end up approving most of them anyway. In organizations with CIO-led governance, many of the hard calls are not made at the enterprise level, resulting in IT leaders having to

TABLE 1-1

Service or control

The line leader wants service.	The enterprise wants control.
I have a great idea for a project.	Yes, but it's not good enough.
The systems need to do a lot.	Yes, but you can spend only a little.
I know what the systems need to do.	Yes, but you need to make sure others agree.
I have a vendor that I would like to work with.	Yes, but you need to use approved vendors.
There's a package that does everything we need.	Yes, but you need to comply with standards.
I'd like to get started right now.	Yes, but you have to wait for resources.
I'd like the project to get done faster.	Yes, but you need to follow processes.
The project just needs a little more time (or money).	Yes, but your time is up, and you need to put the project out of its misery.
The system's ready to be rolled out.	Yes, but you need to comply with the security, regulatory compliance, and business continuity policies.
The system has generated great benefits.	Yes, but you haven't increased your P&L targets.
The system needs to be upgraded (or enhanced).	Yes, but you aren't using what you have.

serve two bosses and fight among themselves and with their business partners about how to best meet the needs of the enterprise and its leaders.

Can We Have Service and Control?

For almost thirty years, IT has been striving to provide better service by improving IT–business alignment, with the goal of ensuring that the right IT products and services are available to meet business needs with minimal angst for all involved.[3] Business alignment is important, but pursuing alignment at the expense of realizing value, running efficiently, and securing the future has a negative impact on the enterprise as a whole. Research indicates that companies that have single-mindedly pursued alignment have lower sales growth and higher IT expenses than do companies having a more balanced approach to IT.[4]

Unfortunately, only 7 percent of organizations have adopted a balanced approach (one that results in higher sales growth and lower IT expenses) given the unwillingness to trade off today for tomorrow. Without a balanced approach that considers long-term enterprise *and* short-term business leader interests, the whole of IT is less than the sum of its parts:

- **Realizing value:** Research proves that companies that are more effective in deploying technology drive higher levels of business performance compared with those that are less effective.[5] IT accounts for half of U.S. capital spending, but only 5 to 10 percent of executives are held accountable for realizing value from IT-enabled business investments.[6] Because demand for new IT-enabled capabilities is seemingly infinite, limited resources must be allocated to projects that have the highest expected returns and sponsored by executives who are held accountable for delivering value.

- **Serving the business:** Creativity and innovation are an art, not a science, with only about 50 percent of IT projects delivering on time, on budget, and on spec.[7] Delivery improves substantially when outcomes are clearly articulated, time is limited, funding is allocated in stages, scope is tightly managed, and skilled resources are assigned.

- **Running efficiently:** Ongoing operational costs account for approximately 71 cents of every dollar spent on IT, limiting the available resources for innovation.[8] By simplifying and standardizing technology, managing vendors, consolidating operations, and automating processes, companies can drive down lights-on costs by 50 percent.[9] (*Lights-on costs* are those that are required to keep the existing technology up and operating and do not include the costs to enhance, acquire, or develop new technology.) These actions not only reduce costs but also improve quality and increase the likelihood that your systems and data are available, accessible, accurate, and agile.[10]

- **Securing the future:** Almost three-quarters of executives believe that IT is a competitive weapon, but a significant gap exists between the perceived importance of IT and the ability to leverage IT to support the key business drivers.[11] It's difficult to foresee future operating imperatives, but the traditional practice of building applications and databases to meet functional needs—rather than to support enterprise business processes and technology standards—has resulted in IT that inhibits rather than enables business change.

Although business leaders evaluate IT on the quality of service delivery, senior executives hold IT accountable for performance across all these dimensions. Kaplan and Norton taught us, courtesy of the Balanced Scorecard, that we don't live in a world of *ors*; we live in a world of *ands*.[12] Competing interests must be reconciled. We need service *and* control. In the world of IT, the competing enterprise interests can be depicted as shown in figure 1-1.

FIGURE 1-1

Enterprise IT interests

Realizing value
How do we increase the
value of our IT-enabled
investments?

Serving the business
How do we improve the
success of our IT-enabled
projects and our change
initiatives?

Running efficiently
How do we reduce our lights-
on costs to increase
innovation capacity and
appropriately manage risks?

Securing the future
How do we ensure coherent architectures
to enable horizontal integration and
promote flexibility and agility?

It's not easy to balance these competing interests. For example, it's tempting to buy a software package to launch a new business without considering whether the technology will easily integrate with existing processes, information, and technologies. Similarly, it's hard to say no to new, promising initiatives when capital funds are available—even though there are few available resources and operating funds are tight. IT leaders can't balance these competing interests on their own, but with support from their business counterparts it's possible to turn "Yes, but . . ." into "Let's go!"

How Can Line Leaders Promote the Enterprise's IT Interests?

You can get IT to work wholeheartedly on your behalf if you understand what drives the enterprise's IT interests and work with

IT to align your proposal to support not only your interests but also those of the enterprise.

- *Realizing value* requires linking your proposal to the enterprise's IT-enabled business strategies and delivering value early and often to justify initial and ongoing costs. To do so, you need to understand the business strategy and IT implications, IT funding plans, the approach your organization uses to evaluate and prioritize IT-enabled investments, and how to develop and deliver new technology so that tangible benefits are realized.

- *Securing the future* entails demonstrating how your proposal enhances cross-enterprise collaboration and integrates critical processes, information, and technology. To do so, you need to understand the target operating model for your business and the implications to processes, information, and technology.

- *Serving the business* is made possible by clearly defining the desired outcomes, delivering value every three to six months, and assigning the best and brightest employees to the projects. To do so, you need to understand how your company manages IT-enabled projects and measures project risk and success.

- *Running efficiently* requires demonstrating how your proposal improves systems performance, reduces ongoing lights-on costs, and helps mitigate operational business risks. To do so, you need to understand what constitutes lights-on costs, how well the current systems support the business, and what plans exist to renew or refresh the existing technologies.

At this point, you are probably thinking, "Are you kidding me? I have a business to run." If you're like most business leaders, you don't know very much about IT and may even resent the implication that you need to learn more, as illustrated by this manager:

> I take offense [to the implication] that management should not only focus on the client's needs, the employees' well being, and maintaining the influx of revenue needed to support the company, but that we should also learn how to do the job of an IT analyst/programmer so that we can better understand the complexities that cause the problems. Isn't that the purpose of having a dedicated IT staff?[13]

To answer this question, let's examine the dismal state of IT-business alignment and why business leaders need to get more engaged with managing the IT assets that fuel their business.

Why Do Line Leaders Need to Get Smarter About IT?

For almost thirty years, improving IT–business alignment has been a top priority for IT. In this quest, IT has been working hard to turn technologists into service-minded business technologists supported by decision-making and delivery processes that are supposed to make it easy to do business with IT.

In spite of IT's alignment efforts, it still has a bad reputation for impeding progress, as illustrated by Gary Hamel's advice: "When you want to run a quick experiment, I tell people don't go through the IT division because they are just going to tell you 'no' and it's going to take forever to get it done." Hamel concludes by saying, "IT has become as much of the wet blanket on innovation as the legal department."[14]

This wet blanket analogy is dead-on, but it's wrong to point the finger solely at IT. There's no doubt that line leaders are annoyed with the predictable "Yes, but . . ." from IT. But it's equally true that IT leaders are tired of being treated like high-priced waiters serving the technology du jour at a moment's notice.

As a case in point, let's review a true story of a midlevel IT leader. Luke has strong credibility with his business partners, as evidenced by the fact that they have tried, on multiple occasions, to recruit him into their organizations. Luke has politely declined these offers, hoping that working in IT will give him the platform from which to drive and enable change.

One day, Luke discovers that his "partners" have unilaterally shortened the duration of a pilot for a new retail distribution system. Surprised, but aiming to please, he adjusts the resources and approach to make it work, albeit at higher risk levels.

Two weeks pass, and Luke finds that his partners have signed a deal requiring rollout of the software to a new customer midstream through the pilot. Going forward with this approach would require Luke's team to work 24-7 for weeks, only to deliver a substandard product. Convinced that this approach would do more harm than good (to the business and his team), Luke decides to throw alignment out the window and proceeds to professionally pitch a fit. He manages to negotiate a compromise, but only after putting on his serious face and making it clear that IT is ready to take its bats and balls and go home.

Luke's business partners didn't mean to cause problems for IT. It's just that in their single-minded pursuit of customers, products, and profit, they simply forgot about IT. In spite of Luke's credibility, his alignment with his business partners looks like the alignment of a husband and wife with separate bedrooms and vacations. And just as weekly counseling sessions and date nights don't heal marital relationships, more governance and processes and metrics won't make a whit of difference in improving alignment between IT and its business partners.

Alignment requires a shared commitment—across IT and the other parts of the business—to assimilate IT into the fabric of the organization. This shared commitment means shared responsibility. IT has spent the past thirty years working on alignment, only to find that when it really matters, alignment exists only on the surface. In essence, IT has been tiptoeing down the hallways in the middle of the night only to find the bedroom door closed. To realize alignment, line leaders need to treat IT leaders as business partners and not simply as service providers.

Are Business Leaders Customers or Partners?

Are you a customer or a partner of IT? If you answered customer, guess again.

Resolving the "service or control" frustration requires that business leaders partner with their IT counterparts to optimize the whole (the interests of the enterprise) and not only the parts (the interests of the business unit or function). As a wise old client of mine articulately states, "IT should be of service, but not subservient."

Of course, it's much more enjoyable, and simpler, to be a customer than a partner. The thought of having to understand the long-term interests, workload, and challenges of my financial planner, gardener, or babysitter is depressing. Why should I? The service is well defined and even commoditized. If my needs are not met, it's easy to pick up the phone and move on. Although some components of IT are of a commodity nature (e.g., computer and network services), the way a business applies technology to support its business processes and impact the performance of its people most certainly is not.

Partners take care of each other. Partners are committed to finding win-win solutions and making it work for the long term. They make sure that their plans, priorities, authorities, processes, and people dovetail. When problems arise, they fight the temptation to place blame and instead examine the context and system that allow great people to stumble and fall.

It's critical that line leaders get smarter about IT and embrace the improvement of alignment with IT as one of their top priorities. IT leaders cannot do it alone. In pursuing alignment, they have almost tied their organizations into pretzels trying to do all this:

- Hire, develop, and reward business and relationship management skills (versus technical skills)

- Assign relationship managers to coordinate and broker IT product development and service delivery

- Link IT and business strategies

- Shift authority for key IT decisions (e.g., funding, priorities, functionality, service levels) to business leaders

- Decentralize application service organizations to mirror the structure of the business

- Improve IT process discipline to clarify respective roles and responsibilities and help ensure consistent, predictable delivery

- Define service catalogs to make it easier for their business partners to understand and request IT products and services

In spite of their efforts over a long period, IT leaders haven't figured out how to insert themselves in a real way in your real world. Every CIO and IT leader worth her weight understands that she should spend at least half her time outside the four walls of IT, working with her business partners to educate, plan, innovate, deliver, and troubleshoot.

When challenged to do so, IT leaders sheepishly admit that they don't know what to do. I have had many a CIO ask me, "What do I say?" as he shied away from spearheading enterprise IT strategy, joint IT–business leadership development forums, IT–business job rotation, and, believe it or not, co-location. To many, these efforts make them feel as if they are inviting themselves to a party where they aren't welcome. IT leaders have done almost everything they know how to do.

As a result, IT feels like a provider rather than a partner. IT leaders are dying for a seat at the table in decision making so that they can advise you about how to get the most out of the systems in place, what technology can do and where it is headed, and how to develop IT-enabled strategy, invest responsibly, deliver complex solutions, and work with IT. Unless business leaders commit to forging a better partnership with IT, whatever is today, will be tomorrow.

As daunting as it may sound, the truth is that business leaders have always wanted more control over IT, as evidenced by their willingness to create shadow IT organizations, select technologies without involving IT, and contract directly with vendors. IT-smart business leaders invest in building strong relationships and teamwork with IT because they understand that IT is an organizational asset, and not simply an organization structure, and that the ability to leverage technology requires effective IT–business collaboration across, up, and down the organization.

What's the New Partnership?

This book is focused on helping business leaders forge a new partnership with IT. Each chapter explores two opposing points of view that express the frustrations of the most disillusioned IT and business leaders. Although the frustrations appear to be irreconcilable, by digging deeper, we can extract, reconcile, and address the two perspectives. Toward this end, this book helps you do the following:

- Focus on relationships to get the results you need from IT (chapter 2)

- Improve strategic positioning through focused, tactical delivery (chapter 3)

- Invest in IT to generate returns sufficient to justify the one-time and ongoing expenses (chapter 4)

- Deliver new IT-enabled capabilities quickly and with quality (chapter 5)

- Ensure that customized capabilities are delivered using standardized, cost-efficient technologies and approaches (chapter 6)

- Foster innovation by effectively navigating the IT bureaucracy (chapter 7)

- Establish the foundation to transform IT from good to great (chapter 8)

The philosophy underpinning the new partnership recalls a line from the movie *Jerry Maguire*: "Help me help you."[15] Partners make life easier for each other while ensuring that their own needs are met.

In this chapter, you've explored the frustration of the seemingly irresolvable paradox between service and control. You can help IT help you by aligning your interests with the interests of the enterprise and working with IT as a partner rather than a provider. Alternatively, you can expect IT leaders to help you help them by establishing transparent IT governance that clarifies and streamlines IT decision making and creating a business- and service-oriented IT organization.

2

You Need Results, and IT Needs Respect

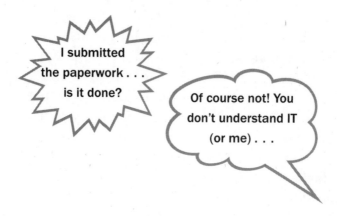

Dealing with a typical IT department is like trying to date someone difficult. There's the promise of something life-changing, but the day-to-day realities are painful—always too little, too late, for too much. It would be great to take a vow of IT celibacy, but in an information-intense, connected world, there's too much history and too much potential to simply walk away.

Some business executives have tried to bypass IT and create relationships with vendors, consultants, and outsourcers. But over time, business leaders have found that even though their words said "partner," they were interested in only one thing—taking the company's money. Others have tried to bully IT into giving them what they want, only to have the smart folks in IT tie them up in knots with passive-aggressive ploys involving governance, architecture, and compliance. Many a line leader has contracted directly with a technology vendor only to come back to IT, hat in hand, after realizing that the road to mandated, secure computing resources leads solely through IT.

There is no way out. You are stuck trying to figure out how to build productive relationships with IT. I know, I know. You've tried to be a good partner by going along with all of IT's processes—from submitting initiatives for financial planning to preparing and presenting business cases for project approval, assigning resources to jointly manage projects and serve as subject matter experts, submitting to the authority of architectural and risk management committees, defining service level objectives, and educating your staff members on the systems they use.

But consider: are you focused solely on results, or on connecting with the people who get the results? The combination of the head *and* the heart is the secret to getting what you want out of IT. The head stuff is straightforward, but the heart stuff is another matter. Relationships between IT leaders and line managers are often strained. The work is inherently complex, and the risks and costs are high.

When you combine the difficulty of the work with the differences in personalities, backgrounds, and incentives, it's easy to see why it's hard for IT and line managers to feel the love:

- As far as personalities are concerned, if men are from Mars and women are from Venus, then IT people are from

Microsoft and their business partners are from Apple. As Paul Glen and his colleagues say in *Leading Geeks,* "Geeks are different than other people." How so? In general, they are "relatively timid and quiet people" "who are more captivated by technique than application" and more aligned and affiliated with each other and their technology than they are with the company in which they work.[1]

- In spite of great effort on the part of IT to become more business-smart, business and IT professionals have very different backgrounds and experiences that make it difficult to communicate what they do and why and how they do it.

- Different pressures and incentives further increase the difficulty of forming positive IT-business relationships. Whereas line managers need to "get 'er done now" to support the needs of their business units (or pay the price in near-term business results and bonuses), IT managers need to "get 'er done right" to support the longer-term needs of the enterprise (or pay the price in fragmented, fragile, hard-to-change systems).

The People Behind the Process

Of course, processes don't get results; people do. IT folks hate the bureaucracy almost as much as their business counterparts do, with 51 percent of business leaders believing that IT is overly bureaucratic and control oriented and 37 percent of IT leaders wholeheartedly in agreement.[2] By their nature, IT professionals are full of "curiosity and playfulness" underscored by a "strong rebellious streak" and a tendency not to "accept leadership easily" and to be "suspicious about the motives of those who would direct them."[3] Although they understand the rationale behind the rules, many in IT believe that the process pendulum has swung too far. Listen to their frustration:

> *There are many in IT who "haven't really DONE anything in years because bureaucracy and process essentially forbids them from doing anything hands on."*

> *"Need hip boots just to wade your way through the rules and the policies."*

> *"The introduction of black holes such as Sarbanes-Oxley . . . has hamstrung IT from doing its job and has ruined what was once a challenging and rewarding career."[4]*

Take advantage of the mutual hate for all things bureaucratic by working with your counterparts in IT to make the system work for you rather than against you. To do so, build strong relationships with the right people in IT, first by understanding the organization.

Who's Who in the Zoo?

If you check out a typical IT organization chart, you'll find something like the one shown in figure 2-1.

The work of IT is organized into three major functions, roughly consistent with the IT supply chain: "plan, do, and run."[5]

- **Plan:** The *office of the CIO* (also called the *IT business office* or *program management office)* is a centralized staff function whose sole purpose is to protect the interests of the enterprise by working with senior executives to define and facilitate IT governance. You may not find a box called "office of the CIO" on the organization chart, but you will

FIGURE 2-1

Typical IT organization chart

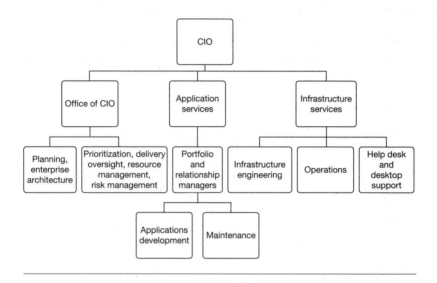

find its component parts: planning, enterprise architecture, prioritization, delivery oversight, resource management, and risk management.

- **Do:** The *application services* group develops new applications and maintains the existing application portfolio. Usually, the structure of the apps group mirrors the business, but, more and more, this group is organized by key business process.

- **Run:** *Infrastructure services* engineers and operates the infrastructure technology (the underlying software and hardware necessary to run the applications). This group also provides end user support, such as help desk, education, and procurement to anybody who uses the company's technologies.

The majority of IT organizations are structured using the federated model to balance enterprise and individual interests. In the *federated* model, activities of the office of the CIO are centralized (to ensure control); infrastructure services are centralized (to capture economies of scale); and application services are decentralized (to improve service delivery to business units).

Outsourcing in IT (and in other functions and processes) has increased dramatically, and, as with anything in life, there are those who do it well and those who are still finding their way. Among my clients, about half of the IT-related work is performed by employees and the rest by independent contractors, consultants, or outsourcing companies. Who does the IT work should not be your decision, concern, or problem. Instead, you should focus on whether you have the right people to get the job done. If you don't, you need to take it up with the powers that be in IT.

Although it may appear that IT has a bazillion employees and should be able to respond to requests on a moment's notice, keep in mind that, on average, 55 percent of IT human resources are needed to maintain, operate, and support the existing systems, and 10 percent are dedicated to office of the CIO activities, leaving only 35 percent for developing new applications, with each developer typically working on a number of projects at any one time.[6] The challenge of finding ways to increase resources focused on development is critical, as discussed in chapters 6 and 7.

Who Do I Need to Know?

The most important person you need to know is your IT relationship manager, who will help you understand, get introduced to, and collaborate with the IT organization.[7] *Relationship managers*, also called *account* or *portfolio managers*, are typically found in the application services group. Relationship management may not be a stand-alone position but a responsibility assigned as part of another job (e.g., IT functional leadership).

If you are trying to find your relationship manager and people look at you funny when you use the term, just explain that you are looking for someone to help you plan your IT needs and get them approved, scheduled, and resourced. If IT has not designated responsibilities for relationship management, request that it do so, and if for some strange reason it doesn't, assign someone from your group to fill the role.

IT-smart business leaders understand that there is no easy, single point of contact, one-stop-shop way of working with IT. Although most IT organizations have a relationship manager assigned to each business unit (or function or business process), there are a whole lot of you and very few of them. At best, relationship managers are effective in facilitating plans, priorities, communication, and relationships, but in no way can they be involved with or knowledgeable about every project, technology upgrade, operational glitch, or help desk call.

Many business leaders at a peer level to the CIO expect him to serve as their personal IT concierge and resent having to work with lower-level IT resources. If this describes you, get over it. It's all CIOs can do to manage relationships with the C-suite and the board and make sure their direct reports are pointed in the right direction. They will be nice and polite when you call and will never say no, but they will turn you over to one of their folks as quickly as possible.

Once you identify your relationship manager, ask him to introduce you to the key people that make the IT organization rock 'n roll (or stumble 'n stutter, depending on how well things are going). To connect with the desired part of the IT supply chain, follow these tips.

- **Planning:** Get to know the leaders in the office of the CIO, because they coordinate strategic and financial planning, define and run the governance processes, and oversee the projects. In addition, develop relationships with the members of the key governance boards (demand management, architecture, project management, service management, and risk management) or their chief advisers.

- **Building:** Spend time with the application and infrastructure leaders, because they significantly influence how projects get sequenced, resourced, and delivered. Also, find the great project managers, business analysts, and engineers so that you can lobby for the best resources. Last but not least, get cozy with the people who maintain and support the systems that your people use.

- **Running:** When you're developing relationships with the infrastructure service leaders, make sure you meet those in charge of quality assurance and change management, because their groups are key to getting approval to move your technology from development to production. And spend time in and around the help desk, getting to know the people who support your technology, because they serve as the gatekeepers to getting your operational issues and service requests prioritized and communicated.

If you have been around the company for a while, you have probably interacted with these people in meetings but you likely don't *know* them. Many of us get trapped in the daily grind of business and focus on the tasks that need to get done rather than the people who do them. Collaborating effectively requires that you understand not only the organization but also the objectives, challenges, values, and motives of the people working within it.

What Makes IT People Tick?

In general, IT professionals "are highly intelligent, usually introverted, extremely valuable, independent-minded, hard-to-find, difficult-to-keep technology workers who are essential to the future of your company."[8] When you find them, remember that, like you, they walk in every day to do the best job they can. Most people are born motivated, and your job is to not demotivate them. To avoid that, you need to understand their core motives.

To Be Challenged

Although IT work is challenging, it's also overwhelming given that there's too much demand for the available supply. Listen to what some IT folks would like to say to you:

"What's your goal, priority, or vision? How can we find ways to take part in it when it only seems to be communicated telepathically?"

"Get a clue on what your system is supposed to do before you just computerize it. Why speed up a disorganized mess?"

"Large companies typically run their IT guys seventy to eighty hours a week with no overtime."

"The real issue is utter lack of foresight by management rather than any kind of Nazi IT Department."

"Imagine twenty different people demanding twenty hours of your time every week. That is IT."[9]

There are an infinite number of ways to apply technology, so before you turn to IT get on the balcony and make sure your ideas make sense from the perspective of your boss's boss. If she would be excited, then you can be assured that IT will be excited as well, because technologists find meaning in the impact that their work has on the customer and on the way the company operates and performs.

To Be Respected

Respect comes from a sense of fairness, trust, and appreciation, and, without a doubt, IT professionals feel underappreciated. Listen to what they have to say:

> *"The majority of IT professionals agree that it's a thankless job with little recognition from nontechnical users."*

> *"You took away half of the dept's jobs and gave them to a team in another country without our consent—despite knowing there is a twelve-hour time difference—and now [you] expect us to teach them the ropes when neither of us can speak the other's language."*

> *"When I was in IT, it was exceptionally clear to me that only two grades were possible. If everything went according to plan (and it never does), you received a C, as this is what is expected. If anything went wrong you received an F."*

> *"When's the last time you thanked your IT staff for taking care of the problem?"*

> *"You did not listen, and then you complain."*

> *"Trust your employees, not the salesman who is buying you drinks on the nineteenth hole."*[10]

IT professionals are smart and educated, and they believe that they should have a voice in key decisions. They put more faith in meritocracy than hierarchy, and you can demonstrate respect by giving your IT counterparts the seat at the table they desperately desire. Because IT leaders are accustomed to business partners calling only when they need something, surprise them by opening the doors to your organization and inviting them to be involved in strategy making and in every aspect of operations—even when it seems wasteful or slow to do so. When decisions are made—in the plane, in the hallway, or in a rush between meetings—stop and consider what's in the best interests of your IT partners. Articulate your goals, and then listen to their ideas and incorporate them in your recommendations. And finally, include your IT professionals in your celebrations, and let them know how much you appreciate them through appropriate, sincere praise and unsolicited favors.

To Be Connected

Connecting starts with understanding and empathizing with others. The more time you and your team spend with IT leaders, the more you will understand their world and they will understand yours. Familiarity doesn't breed contempt. It breeds empathy and understanding—the foundations of good relationships. As it stands, IT professionals don't believe that business leaders are interested in learning about IT and hearing their points of view:

"You show up to a meeting after a chat with your twelve-year-old bursting with new ideas about technology you don't understand and expect us NOT to treat you with condescension?"

"I would expect the management of any company, large or small, to have some technical skills beyond the On/Off button."

"IT sucks because the IT department works for business folks who either don't know what they want or don't know how to communicate it!"[11]

Your efforts to reach out will be noticed and appreciated. Once the IT staffers recover from the shock of your showing up in their office or cubicle (when was the last time you dropped by to visit someone in IT?), ask them, "What do you want me to know? What's going well and not so well? What are our opportunities, and what do you want me to do differently in the future?"

Listen to their answers, and explore root causes. Try to see things from their perspective, and then share what's going on in your world. When the time is right, agree on what your respective teams are going to do differently (the "stops, starts, and continues"), document the decisions and plan of attack, and schedule a series of ongoing dialogues with your teams to gauge the process and maintain focus.

As you interact with IT professionals, approach relationship building as an end in itself rather than a means to an end. Unless you have a sincere desire to tune in and understand their world— what they love, what they want to accomplish, and what drives them crazy—and are willing to compromise and protect them when times get tough, you will be viewed as a self-serving fraud and will be wasting your time.

What's the New Partnership?

In business, as in life, you get what you give. If you try to throw your IT work over the wall with little thought about the people on the other side, you will find, more often than not, that whatever comes back will fall far short of expectations. Capture IT leaders' heads and hearts, as well as their hands, by demonstrating that you are committed to the relationship. Help IT help you by doing the following:

- Treating your relationship manager as a member of your own team (and assigning someone to fill the role if IT cannot)

- Connecting with the people in IT who facilitate the demand management process, support your business and systems, and manage and lead change

- Helping ensure that the people you work with in IT feel challenged, respected, and connected.

As you work to deepen your relationships, expect IT leaders to help you help them by assigning relationship managers to coordinate IT service delivery, hiring professionals whom you respect and like to work with, and devoting at least 50 percent of their time outside their organization to working with you and your team.

3

You Need to Focus on Tactics, and IT Needs Strategic Alignment

None of us likes to be told how to get our job done. And the creative, well-educated problem solvers in IT hate it more than most. If you want IT leaders to support your every whim (or, more realistically, given the overwhelming demand for IT services, even one of your whims), it's imperative to collaborate with them during strategic and tactical planning. *Strategy* is a carefully designed plan of action to achieve an important goal, and a strategy that has broad buy-in will allow you to take control of your destiny and help you secure the resources necessary to transform plans into reality.

The endgame isn't simply about getting along better with IT; it's about expanding your strategic impact. IT not only supports the execution of business strategy but also expands strategic options, as demonstrated in the early days by American Airlines and Frito-Lay and more recently by Walmart and Amazon.com. IT-smart business leaders view IT as a competitive weapon and understand the importance of integrating business and IT strategy development, with almost half of them identifying IT needs when they develop business strategy (in comparison, only 10 percent of IT-dumb business leaders do so).[1]

What Strategy?

Did I hear you whisper, "What strategy?" When asked about their strategy, many leaders sheepishly try to pass off a list of annual objectives or key initiatives and hope that the discussion ends there. When asked to articulate what the future will look like two, three, or five years down the road, many a leader responds with words to the effect, "I know what it is, but I just can't quite put it into words."

Strategy making is a moving target in a complex and changing world, and it's easy to let the drumbeat of demands overwhelm our calendars and our ability to see beyond the short term. Many leaders have a jaundiced view regarding strategy, because they don't see high-level strategies drive day-to-day decision making. In general, only 45 percent of executives are satisfied with the strategic planning process, and only 23 percent indicate that major decisions are made in accordance with strategies in place.[2] The real value of strategic planning should not be judged by whether plans are executed exactly as written. Rather, the impact is in improving the quality of daily decision making so that tactical execution is strategically grounded.[3]

Who's Responsible for Strategy?

It's your job. Leaders want strategic clarity, but they tend to expect it to come from above or outside rather than from within. When it comes to IT-enabled strategy, each party is waiting for the other to make the first move, as shown in table 3-1.

Rather than wait for a formal invitation, you should take the initiative to fill the strategic void. Although I have spent the better

TABLE 3-1

Who should involve whom?

Business says IT leaders should . . .	IT says that business should . . .
"Partner more with the business to identify how technology can be strategically deployed for the business."	"Involve IT as early as possible when contemplating changes to the business or new initiatives."
"Set common goals for long-term business initiatives and the technology supporting them."	"Involve IT early and strategically."
"Get more involved in the early stages of developing strategy."	"Bring in IT early; initiate frequent strategy discussions."
"Be involved in the strategic meetings within all aspects of the business."	"Collaborate with IT to develop strategic and operating plans."
"Offer visioning workshops to broaden the minds of business leaders."	"Involve IT in strategy discussions."

Source: Susan Cramm, "How IT Smart Are Our Organizations?" Having IT Your Way blog, survey taken April–June 2009, with assistance from harvardbusiness.org.

part of my career exhorting IT leaders to initiate strategy making with their business counterparts, it makes more sense for business leaders to take charge. After all, it's your people, it's your process, and it's your P&L. If you are waiting for your IT counterparts to insert themselves into your strategic planning and decision-making processes at just the right time, you'll be disappointed more often than not.

If you decide to order up IT à la carte, understand that your IT waiter will probably be a little surly, and many items may not be available in a timely manner or may be too rich for your wallet. If you *have* tried to get IT involved to no avail, it's time to escalate the issue, starting with your relationship manager and continuing up the IT chain until you get satisfaction.

Once Again, How Will an IT-Enabled Strategy Help Me?

Many business leaders find it difficult to get IT projects approved, in part because they don't know how to get IT's attention and sell their projects in a way that unlocks the various governance doors that stand between good ideas and the necessary funding and resources. The key to justifying projects is to demonstrate the link between your projects and the strategy of the enterprise.

Of course, it's hard to link to something that isn't written down. "Most corporate strategic plans have little to do with strategy," says Richard Rumelt, UCLA's Harry and Elsa Cunin chair in business and society. "They are simply three-year or five-year rolling resource budgets and some sort of market share projection."[4] In the absence of an articulated strategy, managers use a watered-down surrogate: the list of initiatives that survive the annual financial planning process. These lists do not hold up when placed in front of an IT investment board, where final funding decisions are made. Presented with the list, the investment board is not impressed and demands to understand the strategic and financial justification for the initiative.

Chagrined, business and IT leaders try to frame the list as something that is more salable to the powers that be. What results is a prettied-up list in the form of a PowerPoint presentation of issues, objectives, recommendations, and a prioritized list of projects appended with benefit statements such as "increased customer retention," "better decision making," or "increased sales productivity." Nowhere on these pretty pages can anyone ascertain how these projects will contribute to value, agility, cost performance, or growth.

In an attempt to appease all involved, investment boards adopt the deck of cards approach, dealing out project approvals based on politics and backroom deals with the players until the cards run out and funding is depleted. Unfortunately, the resulting enterprise IT list has as much to do with making IT matter as a series of home improvements does to creating a pleasing and functional décor.

Your challenge is to derive and articulate the enterprise's IT-enabled business strategy and link your proposals to it. If you do that, then when the cards are dealt, the investment board will be so impressed with your display of strategic insight that you'll increase the odds of getting what you need when you need it.

How Do I Determine If an IT-Enabled Enterprise Strategy Exists?

To find out whether an IT-enabled enterprise strategy exists, connect with your IT relationship manager and meet the people in the office of the CIO who are involved with planning and getting investments approved. Ask for a copy of the planning documents. If they laugh or hand you a list of high-level objectives, a project road map, or financial projections, you know that no such plan exists and you need to derive one.

On the other hand, if they seem pleasantly surprised by the request, you are probably one of the few (if not the only) business leaders who have asked, and your credibility has just gone up. If they hand you materials that include those shown in table 3-2, you may have something of real value that can be used to justify your IT-enabled business initiatives.

TABLE 3-2

Components of an IT-enabled business strategy

Component	Details
Business strategy	Business goals, including strategy, value chain, business drivers, key technology enablers, and business expectations of IT
Current IT assessment	IT Balanced Scorecard assessment, current architectures, key initiatives, and financial trends
IT strategy	IT-enabled business strategy, including IT objectives, architectures, implementation road maps (applications, information, services, infrastructure,[a] organization), and financial and HR projections
IT plans	Implementation considerations, including oversight, accountability, and success measures

a. IT infrastructure is the enterprise-wide "interconnection of communications networks, computers, databases, and consumer electronics that make vast amounts of information available to users," http://www.techdictionary.com/search_action.lasso?-Database=db_A00534&-Table=Layout+%231&-ResponseAnyError=%2Fsearch_error.lasso&-OperatorLogical=OR&-Operator=eq&-Token=-Search&term=infrastructure.

To determine whether the strategy drives decision making, test your relationship manager for understanding. If she doesn't know what's in the plan, you need to derive the "real strategy." Although the documents may have some good information, they're not commonly understood and will not be much use in getting your initiatives approved.

If you are living a blessed life, you will find that IT has worked with the company's senior executives to define an enterprise operating model and supporting architecture. The operating model defines, at a high level, how your company plans to deliver projects and services to its customers in a way that will ensure competitive differentiation. The supporting architecture details the end-to-end business processes, information, data, applications, and technologies necessary to support the operating model. To learn more about why an enterprise operating model and architecture are so important, read "The Benefits of an Enterprise Operating Model and Architecture."

THE BENEFITS OF AN ENTERPRISE OPERATING MODEL AND ARCHITECTURE

Without a concerted effort to keep things clean, what was once neat and tidy becomes marred and messy. In a typical garage, for example, finding something is like going on an archeological dig. Periodically, when someone dies, relocates, or becomes disgusted, there's a whirlwind of activity to purge and reorganize. This cathartic experience is followed by a brief period of exhilaration, only for the force of entropy to exert itself once again as time passes.

In business, a good example is the airlines. They didn't intend to end up with "multiple old computer systems that don't share information well."[a] When these systems were initially constructed (in the 1960s and 1970s), they were neat and tidy, with application requirements defined from the point of view of a department and the needs of the people within it. The approach to technology development reflected a simple and static world where it was the norm to embed data and business rules together with the logic necessary to support a business function—for example, to book and manage reservations.

No one imagined that customers would book their own travel, airlines would merge and spin off, competing airlines would sell seats through code share agreements, or competition would become so fierce as to necessitate greeting customers by name or remembering their favorite drink.

To respond to these demands in a timely manner, IT did what we all do. It packed as much as it could in the existing "application" garages. When it became impossible to enter these apps without breaking something, IT built new ones to store additional, and redundant, data and business rules. In an attempt to coordinate these applications to support business processes, IT built a myriad of point-to-point interfaces between the applications.

As a result of these seemingly efficient but shortsighted approaches, the architecture of the average twenty-year-old company looks a lot like the garages, closets, cabinets, and drawers in a typical home. The prospect of finding something evokes so much fear that people tend to do without or buy another one.

Because of increased complexity, many companies are in the same situation as the airlines: they don't have a definitive understanding of their customers, products, and performance and have difficulty modifying business processes in response to new opportunities and competitive realities. Furthermore, they spend the lion's share of their IT budgets maintaining existing systems rather than innovating new capabilities.

This isn't new news, of course. During the 1990s, everyone started to realize that IT systems often inhibited rather than enabled change, and, since then, IT and business leaders have been working hard to simplify their architectures by replacing systems and using new approaches that promote integration and commonality. Along the way, we've learned a lot:

- Across-the-board "scrap and rebuild" of systems usually doesn't make sense, because often the gain isn't worth the pain. This approach is like knocking down your garage and throwing out everything in it. There's a lot of good stuff in your existing applications, and there is no guarantee that the new systems will be much better, less complex, or cheaper than the old ones.

- Hiding the complexity of existing systems using a "layer and leave" approach makes it easier to use and integrate existing systems, but it doesn't reduce the costs of supporting inflexible and redundant systems. The "layer and leave" approach is like hiring a garage concierge to find things and put them away. Unfortunately, you have to pay for the concierge service as well as the costs of maintaining the garage.

- The best way to manage complexity is to "clean as you go." This tactic, a combination of the two approaches, is implemented on a project-by-project basis. Each project is defined in a way that moves the enterprise closer to the desired architecture. Using our garage analogy, whenever you move something in, you must reorganize or move out one or two other things. This approach includes layering, but also extracting, critical data and functionality from applications and rebuilding them so that they can be managed as an enterprise asset.

If you aren't careful, existing technologies will become marred and messy. To clean as you go, everyone must agree on what *cleaner* means. For IT, *cleaner* is defined as whatever helps progress toward the company's to-be enterprise architecture.

The *to-be* enterprise architecture defines the processes, data, and supporting technologies that are necessary to support the company's targeted business operating model. *Enterprise architecture* defines not only the goal—the to-be state—but also the current, as-is state. Also included is a high-level road map or plan to get from the as-is to the to-be and how, from a governance standpoint, the organization will ensure that all the players clean as they go.

When companies develop enterprise architecture capabilities, they move through four stages of learning: localizing, standardizing, optimizing, and reusing.[b] Companies in the localizing stage usually aren't even interested in spelling *architecture,* whereas those in the stabilizing stage are focused primarily on technology architecture. Companies in the optimizing stage are serious about enterprise architecture and, if successful, develop capabilities that allow them to move into the reusing stage, when IT-enabled capabilities start to pay off in a big way.

The big payoff in the reusing stage comes from repurposing existing capabilities to accelerate as well as rapidly propagate proven innovations. Unfortunately, only about 2 percent of companies have reached this final stage.[c] Companies struggle with defining their operating models and target architectures and reining in the various players to prioritize the long term over the short term and enterprise interests over those of individuals. That's because what's better for the enterprise over the long term is often at odds with short-term business goals and profitability. The clean-as-you-go approach usually entails additional time, effort, and resources but will save time and money in the long run.

IT isn't alone in the need to simplify. As Harvard's Rosabeth Moss Kantor has pointed out, "Companies sow the seeds of their own decline in adding too many things—product variations, business units, independent subsidiaries—without integrating them."[d] Keep in mind that, because IT architectures mirror the inherent complexity of the businesses they support, it's impossible to have an easy-to-change and cost-effective IT architecture without a simplified business architecture. It's hard to say no to the extra product line, merger, reporting package, or, for that matter, bicycle. As it turns out, simple is not that simple.

a. Scott McCartney, "Your Airline Wants to Get to Know You," *Wall Street Journal,* April 24, 2009.

b. Jeanne W. Ross, Peter Weill, and David C. Robertson, *Enterprise Architecture as Strategy: Creating a Foundation for Business Execution,* (Boston: Harvard Business School Press, 2006), 9.

c. Peter Weill and Jeanne W. Ross, *IT Savvy: What Top Executives Must Know to Go from Pain to Gain* (Boston: Harvard Business Press, 2009), 81.

d. Rosabeth Moss Kanter, "Simplicity: The Next Big Thing," the Change Master Blog, http://blogs.harvardbusiness.org/kanter/2009/02/simplicity-the-next-big-thing.html.

How Do I Derive the IT-Enabled Enterprise Business Strategy?

Rest assured that you are not starting from scratch and won't have to do this on your own. Every business has some sort of strategy, and in your case, it simply may not be written down. To derive enterprise IT-enabled business strategy, first form your strategic planning team. Include someone from corporate planning, your IT relationship manager, a planner from the office of the CIO, and your key leadership team. Next, using figure 3-1 as a template, work with your team to define the approach to deriving strategy that makes sense for you and your company and hold IT accountable for helping you facilitate the process.[5]

As you work through this process, look for existing plans and initiatives that impact the key business drivers shown in table 3-3. Your goal is to close the gap between how important they are and how well they are currently supported by IT-enabled processes, information, and technology.

FIGURE 3-1

Deriving IT-enabled business strategy

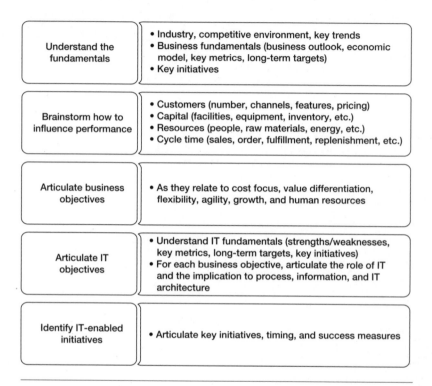

Understand the fundamentals	• Industry, competitive environment, key trends • Business fundamentals (business outlook, economic model, key metrics, long-term targets) • Key initiatives
Brainstorm how to influence performance	• Customers (number, channels, features, pricing) • Capital (facilities, equipment, inventory, etc.) • Resources (people, raw materials, energy, etc.) • Cycle time (sales, order, fulfillment, replenishment, etc.)
Articulate business objectives	• As they relate to cost focus, value differentiation, flexibility, agility, growth, and human resources
Articulate IT objectives	• Understand IT fundamentals (strengths/weaknesses, key metrics, long-term targets, key initiatives) • For each business objective, articulate the role of IT and the implication to process, information, and IT architecture
Identify IT-enabled initiatives	• Articulate key initiatives, timing, and success measures

Keep in mind that IT objectives and initiatives are influenced by the maturity of the IT organization. At the lowest level of maturity, the IT-enabled enterprise plans will be focused on ensuring that IT services and projects are delivered reliably and cost-effectively. More mature IT organizations will extend the value of IT by reducing the operating costs and risks to the business. The most mature IT organizations will further extend their value by impacting the quality of the customer experience and driving top-line revenue.

TABLE 3-3

Importance versus support of business drivers

Business driver	Importance	Support
Lowering the company's overall operating costs	82%	42%
Improving end-user workforce productivity	78%	45%
Improving quality of products and/or services	79%	42%
Acquiring and retaining customers	76%	35%
Driving innovative new market offerings	77%	38%
Managing your customer relationships	73%	38%
Reengineering core business processes	63%	36%
Supporting global expansion	61%	23%

Source: Forrester Research, "The Business-IT Expectation Gap," November 2008, 7. Survey conducted with 600 business executives. Importance reflects percentage of respondents who rated business driver as critically important and somewhat important. IT support reflects percentage of respondents who rated IT support as excellently or very well supported.

Am I Done Yet?

Unfortunately, no—you're not done. Now it's time to demonstrate how your proposed projects support enterprise objectives by linking them to an IT-enabled business strategy *for your organization*. Using the IT-enabled enterprise strategy as context, define your IT-enabled business strategy using this simple process:[6]

Step 1: Assess your current positioning. Do a classic SWOT (strengths, weaknesses, opportunities, and threats) analysis of your business unit operations. Select the top five issues and opportunities for further analysis.

Step 2: Analyze the top issues or opportunities to identify the forces that are driving them. Ask "why?" five times until you get to the underlying causes. At this point you will have five to twenty root causes. Pick the one or two driving forces and explore the capabilities that you will need in the future to improve the performance of your people and processes and the role that technology should serve.

Step 3: Define the objectives and success measurements for each driving force.

Step 4: Define the business unit's IT-enabled strategy by identifying two or three actions that would best address each driving force and would further your business objectives. Map your objectives, strategies, and tactics to the IT-enabled enterprise strategy, and revise as necessary to ensure consistency.

Step 5: Outline how each strategy would be executed, and document accountabilities by using a strategy matrix (with strategies down the left side and business unit or functional accountabilities across the top).

Step 6: Define a project-based implementation road map, including timing, resource requirements, benefits, and high-level accountabilities. Make sure that you spend as much time defining the benefits as you do on the costs and resources.

Step 7: Develop an elevator pitch that summarizes the strategy, remembering that if you can't pitch the strategy, you don't have one. Take the strategy to the streets to gain support of key stakeholders.

Step 8: Secure funding through your company's demand management process (discussed in chapter 4), and implement your strategy using a phased approach, ensuring steady delivery of tangible value (discussed in chapter 5.)

With good facilitation, you can complete steps 1–6 in a few intense days; steps 7 and 8 are ongoing and will never be "done." Be prepared to review progress and adjust plans every three to four months, and repeat the process annually in plenty of time to drive financial planning.

How Can I Mess Up Planning?

If you had to, which would you choose: to be a great strategic thinker or a great strategy maker? The answer follows the same logic as the question, Would you rather be smart or rich? Most agree that it's better to be smart than rich, because smart people can typically make money, but dumb lasts forever. Similarly, being gifted with a strategic mind-set is worthless without the ability to mobilize organizational commitment to the resulting strategy.

When leaders are challenged with developing strategy, time and time again I see the tendency to approach strategy making as an analytical rather than an emotional process. As a result, there is more focus on ensuring the right content than the right commitment.

To illustrate this point, let's look at a typical approach to strategy making. Either by calendar or by inclination, the business leader decides that it's time to develop a strategic plan. She tasks one of her brightest staff members to make it happen within the next month. The staffer solicits input from leaders of the affected functions and defines a scope that is challenging but doable within the prescribed time. Broad participation is required, of course, so the staffer arranges for the leader to announce the initiative as one of the organization's top priorities and to attend the launch meeting.

Now the strategy-making process begins. The plan calls for understanding the enterprise strategy and its implications for the business unit strategy. Once there is a good understanding of the needs at the enterprise and business unit levels, the process shifts to defining how to meet those needs—from a customer, product/service, business process, information technology, human resource, and financial perspective. It all makes perfect sense until theory meets reality: gaining broad participation within the defined scope and time line will be impossible. Everybody is just too busy.

So the staffer makes a critical (and fatal) decision: to shift from strategy facilitator to strategy doer. In this way, the strategy will be completed on time to serve as input to the financial planning process. In the doer mode, the staffer conducts interviews externally and internally and drafts a document that meets the original scope. The leader presents the strategy, and everybody nods his head and gets back to business.

Unfortunately, a lot of effort was expended but little strategy was made. The acid test of strategy is whether it informs and constrains decision making by compelling leaders to align their individual goals and day-to-day decision making to the goals of the business unit and enterprise. The only way to accomplish this is through communication and collaboration. The process of aligning people's hearts and minds is a difficult one that requires ongoing discussion and wrangling. No one can "do" strategy for someone else. It's a leader's job and one that is done collectively, not individually.

Let's help our staffer out and rewind our scenario to the point where it was clear that the strategy process was going to fail. What the staffer needs to do is to open a discussion with the business unit leader about how to complete this iteration of the strategy. Of course, we are talking about reducing scope by identifying the critical one or two issues that need to be addressed (for example, how to share critical customer data across the enterprise).

While we're helping out, let's advise the business leader that she abdicated her strategy-making responsibilities by delegating them to the staffer. The accountability for strategy making is not a staff role but a leadership one. Let's also encourage our staffer and make sure he understands that he has an important role in strategy making. Staff resources should be used for defining and managing the process, coaching others through it, and integrating and overseeing the results to ensure focus and quality.

Those who are strategically gifted tend to emphasize the quality of the idea over the quality of the commitment. But that doesn't work. Never approach strategy making as a purely analytical exercise, and don't trade off gaining emotional commitment in the quest to "get it right" or "get it done." Strategy is never done. In the process of shaping and informing future decision making, it must change to account for the new learning that occurs as those decisions are translated into action.

In summary, making strategy includes a number of key pitfalls.

- **Treating strategy as an event, rather than a process:** Our world is changing too quickly to restrict strategic planning to an annual activity. In reality, strategy is made every day in conversations occurring throughout the organization. A strategic planning process ensures that periodically—every few months or so—the "net out" of these discussions (that is, what is working and not working, how to respond to competitor actions, how to accelerate a successful product launch, etc.) is shared, debated, and documented, with a focus on clarifying what should be stopped, started, and continued.

- **Confusing strategic thinking with strategy making:** Many leaders with huge craniums believe that the ideas are the hard part of strategy making. They are wrong. Cubicles are littered with strategy documents full of promises for the future, held in the hearts of few. Commitment is the hard part of strategy making. To get commitment, you need participation. As Pat Lencioni says, "If they don't weigh in, they're not going to buy in."[7] Remember that strategy is a group sport, and when making strategy, sacrifice completeness for commitment if need be.

- **Delegating strategy making:** Strategy making is the only part of your job that no one can do except you. It's amazing to me how many leaders want to buy a strategy off the shelf by hiring consultants. Hiring consultants to set your priorities is like letting your mother pick your spouse. Input is one thing, abdication quite another.

- **Trying to boil the ocean:** Develop a clear point of view about what's good and what's bad—in and out of your company—by going to the front line of your business and understanding your company from the perspective of your customers, channel partners, and the thousands who serve them on a day-to-day basis. Then define the one or two big things that your organization could do that would have the biggest impact on your business—from the point of view of your CEO or your boss's boss.

- **Separating planning from doing:** Incorporate planning with doing by using your existing governance processes (staff meetings, team building sessions, town hall forums, status reporting, business review meetings, etc.) to develop your plan and keep it alive.

- **Assuming that logic will win the day:** Force yourself to develop the initial strategy quickly, and then work one-on-one and in small group meetings with key stakeholders to revise it until you see their eyes light up. The strategy needs to motivate individuals to trade in their proprietary agendas for a piece of a bigger idea. The vision needs to be articulated in a way that allows everybody to see his ends in your means.

What's the New Partnership?

You can ensure that your IT counterparts will work as your advocate, rather than adversary, by including them in your planning activities. Help IT help you by developing an IT-enabled business strategy for your operating unit that supports the enterprise's goals. Toward this end, expect IT leaders to help you help them by coming to the table and contributing content knowledge (about the IT-enabled enterprise strategy, other business unit strategies, competitors' use of technology, and emerging technologies) as well as process expertise and assistance (including planning methodologies, facilitation, and analytical skills). Providing clarity of purpose to this overcaffeinated world will increase your influence—not only with IT but also with the investment board that stands between your ideas and the resources you need.

4

You Need IT Funding, and IT Needs Returns

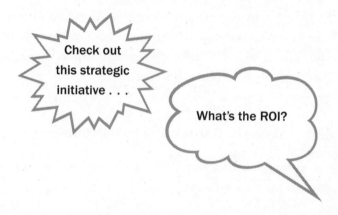

Congratulations! Your hard work is starting to pay off, and your IT-enabled business strategy is gaining traction and getting nods from all the right places—your boss, your peers, the CIO, and the leaders in IT. In your mind, it's time to stop planning and start doing.

Hold on. In reality, it's time to stop planning and start begging for money to turn your ideas into reality. To get funding, you need to navigate the IT demand management process to prove that you're investing wisely in IT. And, yes, the process *is* as bad as its name. Bad, but necessary, given the unquenchable thirst for IT services and that one-half of business *and* IT leaders agree that "the business makes half-baked requests and are clueless about enterprise impact."[1]

As IT becomes embedded within every aspect of a business, there's an infinite number of great ways to apply technology, and a lot of business leaders are competing for the same resources. For years, IT has been focused on narrowing the gap between supply and demand by working on the supply side by improving project management, resource forecasting, process discipline, and flexibility through outsourcing and tapping in to consultants and the contingent workforce. In spite of these efforts, the demand for IT exceeds available supply, and demand management processes are in place to allocate scarce financial and human resources to their highest and best use.

What Is Demand Management?

Demand management is the process of allocating limited resources to the overall benefit of the enterprise. When fully implemented, demand management provides business leaders the information and capabilities to prioritize potential IT-enabled investments, understand related costs and resource requirements, and ensure that these investments drive business results. In short, demand management ensures that the right work gets identified and funded and that it delivers value.

Demand management is a cyclical, reinforcing process that includes the following:

- *Strategic planning* provides the prioritization context for all investments, defining which IT-enabled capabilities are required, how much can be spent on IT, what return is expected, and how IT will be managed to promote and protect enterprise interests while encouraging business unit innovation.

- *Portfolio management* translates strategy into targets for how much should be spent on each of the three types of IT-enabled investments (strategic, enhancement, and keeping the lights on) and, on an ongoing basis, guides decisions and facilitates cross-enterprise project review.

- *Decision rights* are allocated to ensure responsible IT decision making consistent with the principle that business leaders should have the authority to decide *what* IT is needed and IT leaders should have the authority to decide *how* IT is delivered.

- *Financial planning* determines the actual amount of funding available for IT-enabled investments and allocates the funding in budgets consistent with the strategic plan, portfolio targets, and decision rights. In addition, financial planning determines the pricing of IT services and prescribes how other parts of the business will pay for these services.

- *Prioritization* and funding decisions occur on an ongoing basis across and down the organization in line with decision rights and the criteria established during strategic planning, portfolio management, and financial planning.

- *Value management* reinforces accountability for realization of tangible business value by reviewing projections, ascertaining commitments, and monitoring results. This is a critical component of demand management, given that

FIGURE 4-1

Demand management process

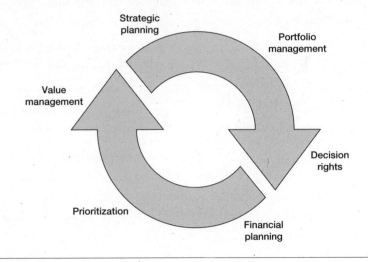

more than 40 percent of business and IT leaders view the ROI from technology-enabled investments as "marginal" or, even worse, view technology as a cost and risk to be managed.[2]

Demand management is a cyclical, reinforcing process in that the value realized from previous IT-enabled investments should inform and shape future strategies, target portfolios, decision rights, funding levels, and so on (see figure 4-1).

As a line leader, you are responsible for developing an IT-enabled business strategy that supports the enterprise strategy, lobbying for funding during financial planning, preparing business cases for prioritization, and realizing value from your IT-enabled investments. The purpose of demand management is to promote responsible IT-enabled investment decisions by encouraging good proposals to come forward while discouraging the "nice but not necessary" ones from seeing the light of day.

As you might expect, companies are at varying levels of maturity in deploying demand management, and it's possible that your organization's leadership has not even heard the term. To determine how to get your projects approved at your company, walk through each step of the process with your relationship manager, starting at the end of the process and working backward.

You're already a pro at strategic planning, so before we discuss how to work the process to get what you want, let's review each step, starting with portfolio management.

Portfolio Management

IT-smart organizations manage demand for IT-enabled products and services depending on the type of investment.

- *Keep the lights on* (KTLO) expenses are necessary to keep the business operating, accommodate business growth, comply with regulatory requirements, and ensure business continuity. KTLO activities include maintaining applications; operating hardware, software, and networks; and providing user support services (e.g., answering calls and provisioning technology.) KTLO spending should be managed for efficiency and is usually centralized to exploit scale economies (made possible through consolidation, standardization, and automation).

- *Enhancement* investments leverage current IT-enabled capabilities by continuously improving the processes, the people, and the technology that support current operations. To ensure adequate investment in strategic initiatives, funding for enhancements should be fixed. To improve responsiveness, it makes sense to give business units or functions authority over enhancement funding as long as they comply with enterprise IT policies and standards.

- *Strategic* investments create new IT-enabled capabilities to improve the company's competitive position. Sometimes these investments are necessary to mitigate a competitive disadvantage (e.g., improve cost structure or customer service levels), to maintain competitive distinction (e.g., continue to empower frontline employees), or to gain competitive advantage (e.g., develop new products). Strategic funding should be managed at the enterprise level to ensure that leadership attention is balanced between today's needs and tomorrow's opportunities.

As with financial investing, each of the investment types has its own level of risk and return, with KTLO having the lowest and strategic initiatives the highest. To ensure that the company can operate in the short term and that it makes the right investments to protect the long-term health of the enterprise, it's important to allocate the available funds across the portfolio in support of the strategic plan. Once the target portfolio is defined, the portfolio is actively managed on an ongoing basis as part of the prioritization process.

Decision Rights

To get your IT-enabled initiatives approved, it's important to understand who makes IT-related decisions and how these decisions are made. IT governance specifies authorities and supporting processes and is critical in protecting the enterprise interests outlined in chapter 1. To put demand management in

TABLE 4-1

Business and IT decision rights

Enterprise interest	Business decides the "what"	IT decides the "how"
Increase the value of IT-enabled investments	What is the right amount to spend on IT, what returns should we target, and what is our target operating model?	How will IT support the operating model, and how should IT be managed to maximize returns?
Ensure coherent architectures	What enterprise-wide processes and information are needed to support the operating model?	How should IT be implemented and organized to support necessary integration and nurture innovation?
Improve the success of projects and change initiatives	What are the essential capabilities, and what approaches will we use to manage change and deliver IT-enabled value?	How will we manage IT-enabled projects and deliver quality solutions?
Reduce lights-on costs to increase innovation capacity and appropriately manage risks	What service levels are required, and what are acceptable levels of risk?	How will we improve services and reduce cost per unit, and how should risk be managed?

context, let's take a moment to review the complete set of IT decision rights.

For each of the enterprise interests, a simple but elegant way to assign decision rights is to grant business leaders authority to decide *what* technology should be delivered while granting IT authority over *how* IT is delivered. At a high level, it works as follows (see table 4-1 for more detail).

- Business leaders should have the final say over IT funding levels and what enterprise-wide and business unit capabilities are required, what approaches will be used to manage change and realize value, and what levels of risk are acceptable.

- IT should have the final say over how to apply technology to create the necessary capabilities given the available funds, how to deliver IT-enabled projects, and how to manage risks and ensure quality, cost-effective services.

There are five types of IT governance (demand management, architecture management, project management, service management, and risk management), and decision rights are managed through governance boards (executive committees, project steering committees, etc.). The boards define the processes, policies, and accountabilities necessary to protect enterprise interests and determine which rights should be retained at the top of the enterprise and which rights should be delegated across and down the organization. IT-smart organizations retain rights involving strategy, investment, risk, and architecture at the top of the enterprise and delegate the management of KTLO to IT, the management of enhancement investments to business units, and the management of initiatives to project steering committees.

When it comes to IT-enabled investments, as a line leader you are accountable for defining what you need, when you need it, how much you are willing to spend, and what value it will bring the company. IT leaders are accountable for defining how to deliver on your needs in the time required and how much it will cost. IT doesn't have the right to tell you what you need, and you don't have the right to tell IT how to do its job, including which vendors, technology, and IT processes should be used. Although the *what* versus *how* delineates who has the ultimate authority, overusing your authority will fracture the partnership with IT. It's better to make these decisions collaboratively, even though it may seem unproductive to do so. Remember, to get buy-in, you have to let people weigh in.

Financial Planning

Now it's time to find where the money for IT is budgeted. As you know, there are two types of financial plans: capital and operating. The capital funds pay for enhancements and strategic projects, and the operating funds pay for keeping the lights on. The capitalization rules regarding IT are complicated, and the way they are applied varies across companies. It's best to leave the accounting to the finance folks and focus on how to bring more cash into the company by increasing the benefits and reducing the costs related to IT-enabled investments.

IT financial planning is typically coordinated by IT, with guidance from finance. The funds are usually managed by IT, so that it's possible for the senior most IT investment board to see a consolidated picture of the IT spend.

- *Keep the lights on* expenses are typically planned in the IT budget. Because KTLO expenses benefit from economies of scale, the rule of thumb is to deliver, or at least coordinate, these services through a centralized, shared service IT organization.

- *Enhancements* are usually planned in IT budgets—either centralized or decentralized, depending on how IT is organized. If you are lucky, the funds have been allocated to each business unit and IT has formed lower-level business unit *IT investment boards* that have the authority to set priorities and allocate enhancement funding, thus streamlining the approval process. If you are really lucky and if IT is really unlucky, investments of less than a certain dollar amount can be approved directly by IT, allowing line leaders to bypass investment boards and go directly to IT.[3]

- *Strategic investments* are typically budgeted at the enterprise level, either in IT or within the operating budget of the sponsoring executive, with prioritization and funding decisions held by the most senior level IT investment board.

Relationship managers work with their business partners to identify anticipated needs for the next fiscal year and lobby the IT financial planner on your behalf. The result is similar to a typical financial plan, with final budgets less than initial requests. Although money is earmarked for IT-enabled investments during the financial planning process, those funds are allocated during the ongoing prioritization process.

Prioritization

At this point, your IT-enabled strategy has sponsorship and the IT budgets are in place. To claim your share, it's necessary to win the hearts of the IT investment board that has authority over your proposed investment. Regardless of the type of investment, your relationship manager should help you navigate the prioritization process. The process filters through the possible investments to identify those with the greatest potential based on the answers to the following questions.

- **Value:** How important is this investment to the attainment of our operating model, strategy, or objectives? How will this investment lessen business risk, and what is its financial return or business impact?

- **Urgency:** How quickly do we need this capability?

- **Initiative risk:** Do we know what we want to accomplish? Is sponsorship in place? Do we have the resources and skills to be successful? Does the project leverage existing technologies and promote target architectures, and is this project dependent on any external factors?

- **Affordability:** Can we afford the initiative?

- **Rank:** How does this proposal compare to others?

- **Commitment:** Are success measures well defined? Have business leaders signed up to deliver the business results, and have IT leaders signed up to deliver within the requested time frame and costs?

To submit your proposal, you need to complete a business case to convey this information to the decision makers. To evaluate your proposal against others, IT will aggregate demand and present it to the investment board as shown in figure 4-2.

To position your initiative attractively, define it as a low-risk, high-value, small to medium-size initiative that is required to support current operations and will help the company progress toward its strategic goals.

- *Manage initiative risk* by leveraging existing technology, demonstrating senior-level sponsorship, and staffing the project with highly skilled, accountable employees.

- *Deliver value* by deploying technology as far to the edge of your company as possible—where the products and services are made, sold, and delivered. The greater the use, the greater the value, so put IT in the hands of your customers, suppliers, and frontline employees, and encourage use by including features that make their lives easier.

FIGURE 4-2

IT-enabled investment portfolio

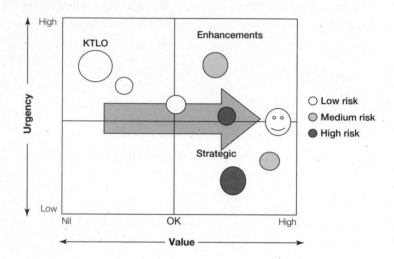

Note: Size of bubble indicates project size.

- *Scope a small project* (completed within three to six months) by focusing on essential functionality, leveraging existing technology, and buying rather than building. If necessary, chunk your initiative into multiple stages and request funding in stages.

- *Support current operations* by delivering near-term value that directly impacts the P&L or drives performance levels, or both.

- *Progress toward strategic goals* by supporting an important IT-enabled business strategy (e.g., promoting cross-business collaboration by sharing or creating common customer information).

IT loves technology and may not give you the cheapest, lowest-risk alternative unless you ask for it. Give IT leaders an idea of what you want to spend based on the projected value of your initiative so that they don't scope out a palace when a park bench will do. Also, make sure they include the total cost of ownership—up-front as well as ongoing expenses—because annual KTLO expenses significantly impact total investment costs. Finally, if the estimates seem high, ask for a second opinion, meeting with external IT service providers if need be.

Value Management

If IT has a dirty little secret, it's this: IT accounts for 50 percent of U.S. capital spending.[4] And even though elaborate systems are in place to show how the capital is spent, few systems are in place to demonstrate that the capital is well spent. In other words, although companies are managing IT spending, they are not managing IT returns. In terms of personal financial management, it's akin to using Quicken to track actuals versus budget but never bothering to run the reports that tally investment returns. Furthermore, if you don't know your actual returns, you can't hold the investment broker accountable for the performance of the portfolio.

Although it seems ludicrous to imagine a meeting with an investment broker that doesn't include a discussion of realized returns, this happens every day in IT prioritization meetings. The typical meeting sequence goes something like this:

- "Exhibit A shows our IT capital budget and allocations to date."

- "Exhibit B forecasts our capital availability."

- "Exhibit C lists project requests in priority order based on strategic fit, value, urgency, and risk. Please note that we recommend investing in the top-rated projects in line with affordability."

There is rarely an exhibit D that summarizes returns and key insights from prior years' investments, expected marginal returns on projects in flight given changes to scope, and recommendations for future funding based on demonstrated impact and business leader commitment to deliver value.

Andrew McAfee observes, "Across the hundreds of quantitative IT business cases I've seen, I'd estimate that the average ROI figure was about 100%." Then he concludes, with a heavy dose of sarcasm, "If this ROI figure is at all accurate, why are companies spending money on anything else except IT?"[5]

Only 5 to 10 percent of companies hold their business leaders accountable for realizing value.[6] That's true even though almost 60 percent of IT and business leaders believe that their ROI from IT is at least acceptable if not good.[7] This is like touting the returns from your financial investments with little proof to back them up.

On the surface, this "managing without measures" approach seems crazy given that businesses are savvy when it comes to managing non-IT capital spending. But this behavior is logical when you consider that most IT-enabled business investments don't directly impact the financials. IT-enabled investments impact financials *indirectly* by affecting the performance of people and the processes they manage. Attempts to analyze the return of a customer relationship management (CRM) system, for example, by analyzing the impact on revenue is an exercise in futility given that there are a jillion things that impact the top line.

Fortunately, the financial impact of IT-enabled investments can be determined by analyzing the relationship between business processes and financial results. For example, a sales support system can lift revenue by supporting process changes that enable cross-channel coordination and improved service levels. Therefore, the returns can be evaluated based on increases in cross-channel sales and reduction of the volume of calls to the customer care center; both measurements have top-line implications that can be calculated directly (in the case of cross-channel sales) or imputed (the impact of improved service on customer retention).

Of course, this approach requires measurement discipline. If your company uses the Balanced Scorecard, you can apply these measures to justify your proposals. Lacking formal measurement systems, you can identify the operational process measures of your business by examining major P&L and balance sheet line items and asking the question, "What drives the performance of this item?"

For example, in the restaurant business, it's possible to increase sales by opening more stores in better locations, increasing store throughput, selling higher-priced items, improving service, improving food quality and appeal, and the like. Once the process measures have been identified, you can use them to justify your proposal and, during development and after implementation, to keep the project on track and validate that value has been realized.

Now, How Do I Get Funding?

To get funding, you need to prepare a business case for review by the IT investment council. Many leaders treat IT business cases as a bureaucratic hurdle (because most companies don't verify that the projected returns were realized), but IT-smart leaders put the business case to good use by using it to shore up support and set up their projects for success.

To build support, align the initiative to the enterprise's strategic business objectives and the selfish interests of the key stakeholders who will be impacted, who will allocate resources, and who hold approval and veto power over the funding. It always surprises me how little leaders know about what motivates the people they hope to influence. To find out what gets them up in the morning, ask stakeholders two simple questions: "What are your objectives for the year?" "What challenges or barriers are standing in the way?" With this information in hand, shape your justification so that they can see themselves in the proposed business case.

To help ensure the success of your initiative, use the business case to drive the focus and approach and to serve as the go-to point of record to manage scope and prove that your investment generated the targeted return. Even though most companies don't measure the returns of their IT-enabled investments, the governance boards are always impressed by leaders who do.

You're Killing Me

I know what you're thinking. There you are, working the front lines of the business, making product, schmoozing customers, and booking sales. In the midst of another busy day, some bureaucrat throws an e-mail over the wall, letting you know that your IT-enabled initiative needs to be better justified.

Within every company, there are IT leaders struggling to make business leaders love them while pushing the bitter pills of enterprise interests. An IT leader doesn't want to make your job harder. He understands that pushing you through governance processes, such as demand management, means pushing you away. But he doesn't have any other choice. He doesn't think you will trade off your individual interests and voluntarily comply with policies and processes that protect the interests of the enterprise.

Sounds silly, doesn't it? Yet every day, business leaders advocate IT investments to support their business units without knowing, or asking, whether the investments make sense when viewed at an enterprise level. More than 45 percent of business leaders admit that they want it all—right now—regardless of ROI.[8] Few business leaders feel that IT is one of their core accountabilities, and "CEOs acknowledge that the governance of IT emphasizes checks and balances more than the strategic use of IT to create value."[9] To shift the focus from paperwork to possibilities, business leaders need to embrace accountability for protecting enterprise interests from within so that governance from above can shift from heavyweight to lightweight.

For now, you are stuck with the demand management process. It's a necessary evil, but you can make your hard job a little easier if you know the rules and know how to play the game. When you propose investments, make sure to:

- *Align* with enterprise strategies and the hot buttons of the key decision makers

- *Enhance* cross-enterprise collaboration and integrate critical processes, information, and technology

- *Deliver* value early and often to justify one-time and ongoing costs and resources

- *Assign* the best and brightest employees

- *Leverage* existing technology, improve systems perform-ance, reduce KTLO costs, and mitigate risks

In everything you do, keep in mind that you want to build a reputation for leading responsibly with IT so that, going for-ward, you are fast-tracked through approval processes.

Should I Just Give Up?

Possibly. As a steward of the company's precious resources, you should be very, very careful to make sure the work you propose is worth doing. According to Peter Drucker, there once was a pa-tron of the arts who told the composer Brahms that he had no in-terest in a protégé "who plays the minute waltz in 56 seconds."[10] Drucker goes on to explain, "In terms of technology, we have people trying to play it in 56 seconds when it shouldn't be played at all. Very little of our computing capacity is well used."[11] If you take a random sample of a typical IT request queue, in my expe-rience at least 50 percent of the requests would bore Drucker senseless because 30 percent of them aren't worth the effort and the rest can be accommodated by leveraging existing systems.

The problem with bad, fifty-six-second IT requests is that they slow down the good ones. Imagine a road with a tollgate. The tollgate represents the IT prioritization process (including logging, defining, estimating, justifying, and evaluating). All re-quests must go through the tollgate before entering the road on their way to their final destination (or delivery, in our case). The bad ideas slow down the good ones by competing for resources and creating congestion that slows delivery overall. It doesn't matter how well tuned the IT supply processes are; too much IT demand has the same impact on progress and innovation that quitting time does on my ability to get home when I'm driving in Los Angeles traffic.

Many an IT investment council has tried, and failed, to reduce IT demand. The problem is that the high number of requests requires too much detailed knowledge to manage IT demand from above. IT congestion can be reduced but only if all drivers do their part. Follow these steps.

1. **Evaluate the idea from the point of view of your boss's boss:** Ask whether the idea directly supports the business strategy and creates tangible business value (e.g., speeds up orders, improves customer retention rate). If the answer to either question is no, make the idea more interesting or walk away.

2. **Check to see whether the capability already exists:** Only about 35% of software functionality actually gets used so it's highly likely that your systems can do more than you think they can.[12] It may be necessary to develop some new skills—for example, learn how to use the data extract and reporting tools—or modify your business process, but it's much faster and cheaper to do it yourself than wait for IT.

3. **Ensure that you are ready to devote the necessary resources:** A project manager and analytical expertise will need to be assigned—from your organization—to define requirements, redesign processes, perform testing, and manage change.

4. **Verify that the idea is as good as you think:** Test or pilot the concept using the available tools (e.g., using a combination

of current systems supplemented with Excel and some manual effort). This approach will not only validate the business value but also highlight any people and process issues that need to be addressed.

The prioritization process works only if business leaders say no to themselves. As an article in *McKinsey Quarterly* succinctly puts it, "The problem is that IT governance systems have become a substitute for real leadership."[13] Leaders at all levels should perform the bulk of IT prioritization on their own before the demand management process kicks in.

What's the New Partnership?

To benefit the enterprise, IT-enabled business initiatives need to be managed like investments. IT-smart companies pay as much attention to the numerator of ROI (the benefits) as they do to the denominator (the costs). Without a balanced focus, the value realized from IT falls far short of its expectations, leading executives to rightly question, "Does IT matter?"

The demand management process rewards line leaders who define IT-enabled initiatives to pay out early and often and who back up their business cases with the commitment to realize tangible business value, in either financial or operational terms (or both).

IT loves technology and wants to do as many projects as possible. Help IT help you by working through the demand management process to gain approval for your IT-enabled business initiatives. Doing so will require that you understand not only the process but also IT decision rights and that you know how to use operational measures to justify proposals, keep them on track, and validate value delivery. IT leaders will help you help them by clarifying the demand management process and decision rights, helping you navigate through the process (including assisting in the preparation of business cases), and ensuring that the mechanisms are in place to track value realized from IT-enabled investments.

5

You Need On-Time Delivery, and IT Needs Quality

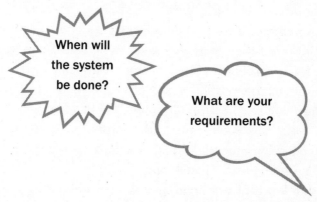

If you think it's tough to get funding for IT-enabled initiatives, it's even tougher to get them "done." It seems easy: you tell IT what you want your new technology to do (your *requirements*), and, voilà, technology is delivered that meets your specs—on time and on budget. No problem, right?

Wrong. IT-enabled change is difficult, and project delivery is pretty spotty. Research indicates that only about half of all projects are delivered successfully (considered on time, on budget, on spec). In general, IT projects tend to deliver too little (about 12 percent of IT-enabled projects are canceled), too late (approximately 33 percent of IT-enabled projects overrun their schedules by an average of 71 percent), for too much (one-third of IT-enabled projects experience budget overruns averaging 41 percent).[1]

Projects that fail are generally characterized by overly aggressive, unclear, and changing aspirations; lengthy timelines; and weak sponsorship and management. When it comes to defining aspirations or requirements, it's easier said than done with one-half of business leaders confirming that they are always changing their minds about what they want their new systems to do.[2]

It's not that business leaders are indecisive; it's just that defining requirements is hard. It entails imagining what can be done and translating these best guesses into excruciatingly detailed, "if, then, else" programming logic understandable by computers. As a result, a large portion of any project consists of IT nagging for requirements. The initially polite "What are your requirements?" question soon leads to the somewhat testy "We don't have good requirements," which inevitably leads to the cranky "The requirements keep changing." With each repetition come increasing levels of exasperation and ever-expanding time lines and budgets. This conversation keeps cycling throughout projects until whatever is being "done" is deemed "done enough," with the funding depleted and everybody eager to move on. At last, another project is "done," evoking a strange mixture of relief and disappointment for all involved.

I love the perspective of Paul Glen and his colleagues on delivering IT-enabled projects: "The point here is not that geeks are incompetent or that geekwork is hopeless, but that creativity and innovation are difficult to do," and "if you expect every project to be completed on schedule and on budget, you're likely to be constantly disappointed."[3]

Why Is IT-Enabled Change So Difficult?

Your left brain understands that there's an ever-present and necessary tension between business and IT leaders that serves to balance the need to get something done and to get it done right. If the relationship is out of balance, IT tends to create short-term, standalone solutions (making integration, information sharing, and collaboration difficult) or, alternatively, overengineered solutions that fail to meet business needs in a timely manner.

But your right brain is perpetually dumbfounded by how difficult it is to accomplish seemingly simple objectives. To understand the challenge of developing new IT-enabled capabilities, let's examine an all-too-real case study of a company that decided to implement common order-to-cash processes in a geographically dispersed, decentralized, service-based business.

Traditionally, each country general manager ran his own show, setting prices, booking orders, deploying resources, providing post-sales support, and closing the books. The corporate office set strategy and annual objectives, developed new services, coordinated global delivery for large customers, and consolidated the financials each month. As competition escalated, however, it became clear that the company needed better information and control over pricing and profitability of orders and customers.

A decision was made to implement an enterprise resource planning (ERP) system to support the standardization of the order-to-cash processes across the company.[4] Long story short, this ERP story ended like many others, blowing by time lines and budgets by a factor of 2.5. ERP systems are notoriously late and over budget given the scope and scale of the business process change, compounded by the difficulty of getting people to use the software to improve the way they do their jobs.

The project sponsor—let's call him Alberto—had prior experience in implementing ERP systems but decided to let the project proceed without using tried-and-true approaches proven to buy down risk and increase the chance of success. Research indicates that it's possible to reduce the risk of project failure by *half* by defining clear business objectives, securing strong executive support and project management, and ensuring sufficient involvement by business subject matter experts.[5] Of course, no one in his right mind would decide to do a project without any of these critical ingredients in place, but life makes us all go crazy from time to time. Alberto lost sight of the big-picture business objective and rationalized that he could sponsor the project in place of a missing-in-action CFO, manage the project personally rather than hire an experienced, full-time project manager, survive with "B" and "C" subject matter experts, and force acceptance of redesigned process changes using a "yank the bandage off" approach.

Alberto proved to be mistaken. The implementation of the system created turmoil within the company, with frontline performers unable to fulfill their responsibilities, challenged by the new software, partially defined processes, and missing and inaccurate data.

Alberto left the company shortly after the initial implementation. He didn't get fired, but his reputation was damaged and he left exhausted and disillusioned. Alberto is proof positive that even though it's important for change agents to be fearless, it's a good idea to take out some insurance so that the job doesn't become fatal.

How Do I Succeed When Others Have Failed?

When planning IT-enabled change, you can increase the odds of success by following these guidelines.

- Define a crystal-clear purpose that works for the business and the people on the front lines (customers or the people who serve customers).

- Engage the head, heart, and hands of your people in the project and change effort.

- Integrate and streamline business processes.

- Leverage existing technology to the fullest.

- Define a fast-cycle approach, assigning the best people and delivering capability every three to six months.

I see a lot of companies investing money in IT-enabled initiatives that aren't ready for prime time. It's not that the ideas are bad—most of them aren't—but they aren't well thought out.[6] Even armed with a clear purpose, everyone (business and IT alike) underestimates how difficult it is to define, in detail, new ways of working and to get people to adopt the new processes and tools. Often, the easiest part of IT-enabled change is building new or configuring existing technology with the hardest part getting people to wholeheartedly embrace the new ways of working. John Thorpe, in his book *Information Paradox*, observed that "initiatives which at first appear to be dominated by technology, on analysis, prove to be exactly the opposite."[7]

How Do I Define a Clear Purpose?

Technology can help us do almost anything. In considering the options, you need to ask the question, "I know we can do it, but should we?" We all use, or rather misuse, smart technology to do dumb things. I've attended meetings in body, but not in spirit, because of the lure of my constantly buzzing BlackBerry. Everyone has diddled with a PowerPoint presentation by spending hours searching for the perfect graphic, adjusting the fonts, and positioning the text. And, of course, most of us have experienced regret and remorse for sending an e-mail late at night in a fog of anger or fatigue.

Unfortunately, our lapses in techno-judgment go beyond the ways we use our personal "productivity" tools. They also are manifested in the systems that we use to run our company's core processes. The impact of doing stupid things to our business far outweighs the impact of doing stupid things to ourselves (given that we personally bear the brunt of these behaviors in the form of poor performance appraisals, long work hours, and strained relationships).

Armed with a good business case, leaders often focus more on technology than on the people who have to use it. Table 5-1 shows a few examples of how good technology can go bad.

These examples illustrate two crucial principles about defining purposes that work for people as well as the business.

- **Equip frontline employees:** When you do this, you increase
  the breadth of IT's impact by pushing technology as
  far down in the organization as possible. The greater
  the use, the greater the value. Don't give decision support
  tools to senior executives, or business process tools to
  an elite group of specialized analysts. Instead, equip the

TABLE 5-1

Bad and good applications of technology

Technology	Done bad . . .	Done good . . .
Customer relationship management (CRM):[a] provides a 360-degree view of the customer	Require sales reps to enter additional data, thus negatively impacting productivity and data quality	Focus on providing tools that increase sales force effectiveness, collecting necessary data as a by-product
Business process management (BPM):[b] improves process effectiveness through measurement, modeling, simulation, and refinement	Redesign business processes using IT and business analysts, resulting in changes that don't reflect frontline realities	Enable process workers and teams to measure, analyze, and refine process performance on a continual basis
Business intelligence (BI):[c] improves decision making through better information	Create a dashboard for top management while expecting the rest of the organization to make decisions using gut and spreadsheets	Identify key decisions and encourage those involved to trade in their spreadsheets for access to clean and easier-to-use analytical tools

a. CRM applications help companies manage customer-related information, match customer needs with product plans and offerings, remind customers of service requirements, identify the other products a customer has purchased, and so on, http://searchcrm.techtarget.com/sDefinition/0,,sid11_gci213567,00.html.

b. BPM systems are a set of software tools that support "process analysis, design, deployment, execution, operations, analysis, and optimization" (Howard Smith, *Business Process Management: A Platform for Innovation*, http://lef.csc.com/library/publicationdetail.aspx?id=5002, November 17, 2005, 14.

c. BI is a broad category of applications and technologies for gathering, storing, analyzing, and providing access to data to help enterprise users make better business decisions. BI applications enable decision support, query and reporting, analytical processing, statistical analysis, forecasting, and data mining. Adapted from http://searchdatamanagement.techtarget.com/sDefinition/0,,sid91_gci213571,00.html.

frontline employees who serve your customers and run your business.

- **Tap in to core motivational needs:** Increase the depth of impact by implementing features that serve the interests of the business and the people within it. Don't expect people to trade their old practices for systems that make their jobs harder or more mundane. Instead, figure out how to tap in to their core motivational needs: to be challenged, respected, and connected. For example, encourage sales reps to enter timely and accurate data by providing something of value in return, such as customized sales presentations, elimination of administrative paperwork, or insights regarding successful sales strategies employed by other sales reps.

When you define the purpose of your initiative, tie it to the IT-enabled enterprise business strategy and scope it to increase the breadth and depth of adoption by adding value not only to the business but also to the people on the front lines who buy products and services or interact with people who do. In addition, translate your purpose into success metrics, including operational process measures (outlined in your business case) and systems adoption (since, without use of the technology, downstream benefits will not materialize.)

How Do I Engage Others in the Change Effort?

Volumes have been written about change. Rather than make a feeble attempt to summarize a complex topic, this section underscores that your most important role on IT-enabled projects is that of a change agent. Even when presented with a dramatic, personal case for action, people don't change; for example, research shows that only 9 percent of patients with coronary heart disease adopt more healthful lifestyles.[8] People spend most of their time operating in the unconscious part of their brains, where behaviors are programmed and automatic. Case in point:

isn't it disconcerting to find yourself five miles down the freeway without a memory of how you got there? To get people to change, you must engage their frontal cortex so that they can re-program the rest of their brains and drive to a new location.

The only way to engage the frontal cortex is to get people actively involved in the change process. When planning initiatives, do so in a participative manner. Sketch out hypotheses (using white-boards, not PowerPoints), leaving lots of white space, and ask questions that invite engagement and challenge ("What's missing?" "What won't work?" "How would you do it?" "What's the next step?"). When you're educating the organization on the initiative and its impact, discard the concept of a communication plan. In-stead, define a "listening plan" to promote dialogue that creates shared understanding and insights about what's going well and not so well and how to tackle the barriers that put the project at risk.

Participation and dialogue will capture heads and hearts, but you need to engage hands to move from ideas to action. Do so by making it easier for people to do the right thing than to do the wrong thing. Simplify processes and jobs, and, because we are herdlike animals, use peer pressure to accelerate adoption by pilot-ing the new system with people who carry a lot of influence. In ad-dition, address the core motivators—challenge, respect, and connection—by making jobs more interesting (by pushing author-ity down, not up), sharing information broadly, and facilitating collaboration within your organization and across the enterprise.

What's Process Got to Do with IT?

IT leaders are dying for you to take responsibility for optimizing your company's end-to-end business processes (versus simply the processes under your control). Business processes are a complicated mess and poorly understood, but they're rigorously defended by the people who make them work on the fly. Overlaps and disconnects are hidden from view because of the siloed nature of organizations. People like what they know, so it's difficult to get them to change their routines in spite of daily frustrations and evidence that they don't make sense when viewed from an enterprise perspective. Process streamlining and standardization—the heart of every IT-enabled initiative—are difficult and complex, because they require bridging the silos and forging a common understanding of what should be, what has been, and how to close the gap.

At the start of every IT-enabled project, devote effort to identify necessary process changes. At a high level, this involves the following:[9]

- *Describe your operations* in terms of desired business outcomes (e.g., to generate demand) and not what people do or how they do it.

- *Identify activities* that support your desired outcomes (e.g., managing partner relationships, marketing services, selling services).

- *Determine the processes* supporting each of your activities (e.g., managing orders, managing sales, and configuring pricing).

- *Identify critical processes* for improvement based on current performance and impact to desired business outcomes.

- *Prioritize process improvement opportunities* by evaluating business impact versus the effort required to improve the process performance.

Some of the biggest performance improvements come from optimizing the business process as a whole (versus the parts), so be sure to look upstream and downstream by analyzing the process handoffs with your internal and external partners.

Now, Can We Talk Tech?

IT-enabled projects aren't easy, but business leaders make them harder than they have to be by ignoring the technologies currently in place and at their disposal. Software is configurable, so when you consider what to change, find out what your current systems can do. It may seem like the tail wagging the dog, but IT capability needs to inform your business plans and projects and not simply treated as an after-the-fact consideration. Ross and Weill confirmed this when they found that companies with highly digitized and standardized business processes and platforms have higher levels of agility—provided that they exploit and leverage these platforms for execution and growth.[10]

Insist that your initiatives leverage existing technology. This is harder to do than it sounds. Although most business and IT professionals worth their weight will agree with this principle, it's hard to resist the allure of bright and shiny new technology and question their optimism in believing that the devil they don't know is almost certainly better than the devil they know.

New technology isn't necessarily better—it's only different—and by insisting on using existing technology, your initiative will be cheaper and will get done faster. Not only will you avoid the effort involved with product comparisons, demos, negotiation, contracting, installation, configuration, and testing, but also you will avoid the unpleasant surprises that inevitably arise the moment technologists rip off the shrink-wrap.

Replacing existing systems is usually a nonstarter unless there is a provocative business case. Systems take a long time to wear out, in spite of being deemed obsolete by the vendor. It usually doesn't make sense to pave the cow path unless you can prove that a new system is the only means possible to get to an important, valuable end. As with the ten-year-old car in your garage, as long as the technology works it's much better to focus attention on where you want to go than how you get there.

How Do Projects Get Done Quickly and with Quality?

Project success declines dramatically as project size increases.[11] Moreover, fast projects are more successful than slow projects. When it comes to IT projects, less is more. While it's true that it takes big money to fix big problems, the way to solve big problems is to solve a series of small ones.

Be sure to break large projects into smaller pieces or stages, with each stage delivering value within a three- to six-month time frame. If you use time as an input rather than an output, your teams will be forced to focus on the practical versus the possible. This pragmatic approach not only simplifies the process of defining requirements but delivers near-term value so necessary to capturing and nurturing the precious organizational mindshare that helps ensure success.

Contrast this with the "boil the ocean" approach. In the futile attempt to define *the* long-term solution, teams mill around smartly, trying to know the unknowable, defining to-be architectures, drafting requirements, and evaluating technology options. In the process, time and money are wasted producing paper rather than performing experiments. If the American pioneers had used this approach, most of the population would still be living in Boston.

Given that only about 35 percent of application functionality is typically used (and you can't predict which 35 percent), it's impossible to figure it all out in advance.[12] The key to bringing the future forward is to get tools into the hands of your people as quickly as possible. If they use them, you are on the right track. If they don't, find out why and give it another go.

This stumbling and bumbling, learn-by-doing approach may seem a little chaotic, but it's reflective of the ways organizations, and people, change and grow. Mistakes will be made, but it's better to make a series of small mistakes and midcourse corrections than to make one huge, multimillion-dollar mistake from which there is no way to recover.

To determine what to tackle first, identify the capabilities necessary to realize the benefits defined in your business case. To realize value quickly, use a fast-cycle development approach where value is kept center stage by addressing the questions in table 5-2 (for a primer on fast-cycle development, see appendix A).

Use your value metrics throughout the project to maintain focus on the endgame. Define the measures as part of developing the business case, baseline the measures during construction, and measure changes during the transition phase, ensuring that the initiative doesn't end with deployment of the system but rather with realization of value after implementation. By managing value throughout development, you increase the odds that the initiative will realize value or, if not, will provide the information necessary to challenge key assumptions necessary to refine the objectives and approach or kill the project.

Although business and IT partners generally agree in principle with the three- to six-month delivery rule, in practice they struggle with fast-cycle delivery for three reasons.

TABLE 5-2

Value-driven development

Project phase	Questions that drive value
Inception (preliminary investigation)	• How will this initiative benefit shareholders, employees, and customers?
	• What key capabilities will be in place once we have successfully delivered?
Elaboration (analysis, design, some coding)	• What must be done to create the new capabilities?
	• Which approaches should we consider, and which one gives us the biggest bang for the buck?
	• How will we measure value, and which improvements are we targeting?
	• How can we approach the project so that benefits are delivered early and often?
Construction (coding and testing)	• What is the current performance of each value metric?
Transition (testing and deployment)	• How have we impacted value?
	• What have we learned that we should incorporate into future stages?

Source: Adapted from David Sward and Richard Lansford, "Measuring IT Success at the Bottom Line," Intel Information Technology white paper, April 2007.

• **The project will appear longer and more expensive:** Breaking a big problem into a series of small ones results in a total duration and budget wherein the sum of the parts *appears* greater than the whole. Of course, this is a fallacy because the chance of success using the boil-the-ocean approach is relatively small.

- **It forces hard choices about what will and will not be done:** Getting approval, funding, and resources takes so long that IT and business leaders are reluctant to eliminate anything from the must-have list.

- **It's harder to deliver the right thing fast than the wrong thing slowly:** Quick delivery doesn't give IT much time to define architectures and develop infrastructures to ensure that whatever is built will promote the enterprise interests of integration and standardization.

To deliver quickly and with quality, ensure that the following are in place.

- **Executive leadership:** If you don't carry the weight necessary to garner resources, make decisions, and cajole people into behaving, make sure you have an executive on board who wants your project as much as you do. Don't simply sponsor the project; lead the project. For example, sponsors show up at steering committee meetings when invited, whereas leaders demonstrate passion and commitment by showing up in cubicles and conference rooms uninvited.

- **Predefined kill switch:** Take the emotion out of the decision-making process by determining the criteria that constitute failure (e.g., the project will be killed when budgets and time lines have been revised twice and nothing has been implemented) so that the project can fail fast and be restarted when conditions are more favorable. As one of my CIO clients says, "A great way to make a project succeed is to kill it."

- **Small, experienced team:** Get the good ones and not necessarily the available ones. Wait to start your project until you have a seasoned project manager supported by a small team (fewer than twelve people) of full-time business analysts, subject matter experts, and engineers. If you don't like the people that IT gives you, select the ones you want and verify that they are available. IT sometimes starts projects slowly because its resources are overbooked (something that a client of mine calls the "false start syndrome"). Just because a hotshot project manager shows up at your door doesn't mean your project has started. If the resources aren't available, ask for some fresh picks, insisting on outside resources if need be. Don't let IT's supply constraints be your problem. There's a whole world of external IT resources waiting to help you, and it's IT's job to ensure that sourcing relationships are in place so that once projects are approved, resources are available.

- **Predefined architectures:** When an initiative comes along, IT leaders should already have a good idea where it fits into the to-be architecture from the process, information, applications, and technology perspectives so that they have the good shot of building it right. Unfortunately, most IT organizations don't have mature architecture capabilities, causing fast-cycle projects to exacerbate complexity rather than reduce it. If this is the case in your organization, give IT a little more time to figure out where your solution fits in, and help the group lobby for architecture resources to alleviate this issue going forward.[13]

- **Off-the-shelf infrastructures:** Oftentimes, the application services folks tell the infrastructure folks which infrastructure they need. This build-to-order approach is slow and expensive and is now being replaced by provisioning standard, off-the-shelf technologies using software that can allocate the resources dynamically based on the application's service requirements. Unfortunately, many IT organizations are still in the build-to-order mode. If this is the case in your organization, let infrastructure services, and not application services, define the underlying technology. Give them a little more time to set up the infrastructure and help them lobby for the resources to establish off-the-shelf capabilities necessary to alleviate this issue going forward.[14]

Once Again, How Do I Get My Project "Done"?

It's no wonder that IT projects often exceed original time and budget estimates. If you corner any IT person over a drink (not a difficult task under any circumstances), you will discover that she is overscheduled and is well aware of the optimistic assumptions reflected in your project plan. Most likely, you aren't asking the tough "what if" questions, and she, in the spirit of "IT–business alignment," has no interest in being the messenger killed with the message. Support your project manager and team by having difficult but crucial conversations to ensure that good decisions are made and that the odds for success are on your side.

Let's reflect on the earlier ERP example. Alberto knowingly broke a lot of rules. He allowed the project to start even though the purpose was fuzzy, the scope was too large, and accountability for process change was not in place. He assumed the sponsorship role for the project when the CFO left for personal reasons. He allowed an inexperienced project manager to be assigned and assumed day-to-day management responsibilities when she didn't deliver—even though he had a department to run. He halfheartedly tried to raise issues but sent mixed signals. In the beginning, he didn't want to sound like a naysayer and kill the project before it began. In the end, he was embarrassed and felt professionally at risk.

Most project managers are well aware of the risks of their projects. Researchers have found five crucial conversations that need to occur to help ensure project success. Unfortunately, only about one in five project managers knows how to effectively engage in the right conversations to mitigate these risky behaviors.[15]

- **Are we planning around facts?** Timelines are set without considering what needs to be accomplished.

- **Is the project sponsor providing support?** Sponsor isn't engaged, too busy, or doesn't understand how to provide IT-enabled change leadership.

- **Are we faithful to the approval process?** Decisions are made without following a disciplined, inclusive process.

- **Are we honestly assessing our progress and risks?** The project team does not know how to access project risks and/or communicate them openly and honestly.

- **Are team members pulling their weight?** Project managers do not have the authority over staffing, directing, and replacing team members.

Constructive, and often difficult, dialogue results in good decisions, and good decisions drive success. Get together with your project manager early and often in informal, relaxed settings, and make it easy for him to surface his anxieties and identify the risky behaviors in play. Provide air cover so that the project manager isn't killed with the message by facilitating the difficult, but necessary, conversations with whoever is standing in the way of progress.

Alberto's ills were self-inflicted. He knew better but did it anyway. Don't let this happen to you. Don't do anything you don't believe in. If someone tries to force your hand, respectfully and humbly decline. As a wise old boss of mine used to say, "It's better to eat it on Sunday than every day of the week." Keep in mind that if your project were easy, it would already be done. The company wants you—needs you—to succeed.

Should I Go It Alone?

IT folks are deathly afraid of rogue IT activities and shadow IT organizations. These ominous-sounding terms call out the nefarious intentions of business leaders trying to hijack IT's decision rights. Don't do it. Once you go astray, you'll never be trusted again.

You *can* go it alone as long as you have IT's permission. You don't have to ask for it directly, but you'll get the nod as long as you solicit IT leaders' advice and invite them to participate. When they respectfully decline because of other commitments, promise that you will keep them informed and pull them in at critical decision points to ensure that the interests of the enterprise are protected. Because IT is embedded in virtually every business process, IT leaders understand that it's impossible to get involved with everything. But they don't want to be the clown behind the circus elephant, cleaning up your mess when you get in over your head.

To exert more control over your IT destiny, build skills that allow your organization to make smarter IT decisions and accelerate IT-enabled change. Doing so will reduce your dependency on scarce IT resources and allow you to assume responsibility for

- Developing IT-enabled strategy and business cases

- Leading IT-enabled business change

- Managing IT-enabled projects

- Performing business process and information analysis

- Fulfilling IT needs through self-service, including using self-help diagnostics to troubleshoot problems with existing systems

- Using the configuration tools available in the existing systems to change processes, business rules, and information displayed, captured, analyzed, and reported

Business-smart IT leaders do everything they can to enable, and not inhibit, business partner self-sufficiency. They understand that this practice will increase innovation capacity and allow IT to focus on higher-leverage activities that will, over time, enhance the perception of IT's responsiveness.

What's the New Partnership?

There are no "IT projects;" there are only IT-enabled business initiatives. Research shows that "around 90 percent of the CEOs expect business units to identify the IT investments needed to implement their strategies; to support, monitor, and assess important IT projects; and to help make IT-investment and budget decisions as well as the process and organizational changes that technology implementations require."[16]

Help IT help you by assuming responsibility for managing IT-enabled business change using a fast-cycle, value-driven approach. Define a clear purpose, assign top-notch talent, focus on the most valuable features, foster constructive team dialogue, and help IT leverage existing technologies, optimize end-to-end business processes, and move toward target to-be architectures.

Expect IT leaders to help you help them by sourcing top-quality talent (project management, business analysis, engineering, and architectural skills) and creating a culture and capability that support fast-cycle, value-driven delivery (including project management and software development processes and flexible sourcing that ensures that once a project is approved, it can be initiated in a timely fashion.)

6

You Need Customization, and IT Needs Standardization

It's graduation day! You and your team have decided that the technology you've been developing is "done enough" and ready to be deployed across the organization. To get to this point, you've worked diligently through the project, architectural, and risk management processes that helped ensure the project was well run and your technology is well built.

To get technology deployed, the powers that be in infrastructure services must agree to move it from development to production. *Production* consists of all the technology that is running your company's current operations. Needless to say, moving something into production without approval is a big no-no. Production is like an exclusive, gated resort where your technology needs a pass to get in, and, once in, it benefits from special amenities, including security, backup, performance monitoring, and 24-7 support.

To get a pass, your technology is subjected to the change management process.[1] The project team must provide documentation that details how the technology was built, proves that the technology was thoroughly tested and in compliance, and explains how it should be operated so that it meets your organization's service level requirements.

- *Testing* is performed by the project team, and, because technologists fall in love with their technology and always think it's perfect, it should also be tested by a quality assurance team that does not work for the project manager.

- *Compliance* with important policies and guidelines should be built into the technology during development, subject to rules defined by the risk management and architecture management governance boards. Risk management governs policies such as security, regulatory compliance, and business continuity, and the architectural review verifies that the technology is designed to promote enterprise integration and reduce complexity.

- *Service levels* are a measure of the performance of a system or service as defined by uptimes and downtimes, repair times, response times, cycle time, quality levels, and so on.[2]

Although it may seem that your poor little technology is being subjected to the whims of a bunch of bureaucrats, this oversight is critical to protect the interests of the enterprise and keep your business operating. Oversight is seldom welcomed, but it is necessary given that "an IT disruption can paralyze a company's ability to make its products, deliver its services, and connect with its customers, not to mention foul its reputation."[3]

Once It's in Production, Am I Finished?

Unfortunately, no. The technology you sponsored into production needs to be operated, supported, maintained, and enhanced. As the owner—an honor bestowed on those brave enough to sponsor IT-enabled initiatives—you are responsible for working with IT to do the following.

- **Educate and hold users accountable for exploiting the technology:** Overall, only a fraction of the available functionality is typically used, and, unless the technology is adopted, the projected benefits will not materialize. Your IT partners and power users can brief you on the features that are being used (or not used or misused) as input to your development plans.

- **Resolve technology issues quickly:** These are documented in incident reports due to issues called in to the help desk or identified during operations by infrastructure services. Once incident is resolved, work with IT to ensure that the root causes of problems are identified and addressed. Usually, these issues are episodic, not chronic. If you find yourself in firefighting mode trying to keep a mission-critical system up and operational, read "Emergency Care for Sick IT Systems."

- **Maintain and enhance the technology to support the changing needs of the business:** Once you and your team start using the new technology, its deficiencies will become glaringly obvious. Although some changes will be mandatory (e.g., compliance reporting), others will not. Be sure to apply the same rigor in evaluating and prioritizing the enhancement requests that you did in scoping the original effort.

- **Secure funding and resources to support all these tasks:** When you develop the business case, be sure to include post-implementation costs and head count requirements. On an annual basis, work with IT via demand management to make sure it has the resources and funding to support and maintain your technology.

Is That All I Need to Know?

Almost. Because graduation days are about reflection as well as anticipation, let's look back on how well our recent graduate—the technology you've just transferred into production—supports the enterprise's interests.

- What was done to ensure that the IT-enabled technology was completed as promised and adopted by the end users?

- What positive impact has the IT-enabled initiative had on the core operating metrics of the business?

- How did the technology help clean up the existing architecture to enable horizontal integration, flexibility, and agility?

EMERGENCY CARE FOR SICK IT SYSTEMS

You arrive early one morning to discover that a mission-critical system, the one that supports inventory fulfillment, is DOA—again. As the system owner, you are on point to work with IT and get this resolved.

It's a sobering reality that many companies face significant operational exposure due to fragile technologies. System downtime or degradation extracts a huge financial toll—as much as 3.6 percent of revenue, according to a 2004 study.[a] And no one is to blame. Over time, every system needs to be modified. These changes are introduced gradually, as small enhancements. Eventually, the functionality of the system is extended far beyond its original purpose and design, causing the system to become increasingly complex and unstable.

You've convened meetings with various overworked IT specialists to discuss how to improve the health of the system. Like physicians diagnosing a rare condition, it's hem and haw. The specialists are reluctant to jump in and try to fix the system, because changes to one part can have cascading, unanticipated impacts to others. Conversations with the IT specialists swirl. They prescribe design modifications, rewrites, application monitoring tools, and process improvements, but the ideas never settle down into a logical treatment plan. And none of these prescriptions addresses the need to decrease outages to a tolerable level—as soon as possible.

Avoid this scenario. Don't get lulled into buying in to a long-term wellness program without first stabilizing the existing system (just as you wouldn't start a running regimen after learning you had a heart condition). You don't need meetings.

You need a mandate and a team of experts focused on your case. You need the organizational equivalent of an IT emergency room.

Here's what to do. Appeal to the CIO to create a dedicated cross-functional team of IT and business specialists. Assign business experts to work side by side with IT experts hand-selected from the various IT specialties, including architecture, development, infrastructure engineering, and the help desk. Ensure that this team reports to you and the CIO. Once the team is in place, make sure it follows these four steps.

1. **Start evaluating the symptoms:** The problems, such as outages, must be documented in incident reports available to everyone on the team. Ideally, the incidents should be funneled through the help desk for initial diagnosis and escalation. If your organization doesn't have trained help desk personnel and disciplined incident and problem management processes, route these calls to the team so that they can document the issues and apply quick fixes to get the system up and running.

2. **Document the related business processes, applications, data, and infrastructure architectures:** The team needs to have a common, big-picture view of what the system does and how it's built. This entails analyzing the business processes and mapping the processes to the underlying applications and data and then mapping the applications and data to the underlying technologies. Without this perspective, it's impossible to diagnose and rectify issues. You'll quickly discover how little collective intelligence

exists about critical processes and systems that have been around for years.

3. **Conduct differential diagnosis:** Analyze the incidents to identify root causes and prioritize fixes based on business impact. Over time, the team will see patterns emerge (e.g., problems occur at month end, when volume reaches certain levels, when data contains certain values, etc.).

4. **Implement the changes:** To protect against the likelihood of introducing more problems and instability, test the changes in an environment that mirrors the one driving the production system.

Continue steps 2 through 4 until the outages reach an acceptable level. Once you define an ongoing wellness program that ensures regular monitoring of system performance, you can disband the dedicated team. Then start developing a business case to replace the existing system. Keep in mind that the goal is not to replace the existing system in kind, but to identify business process changes that will make fundamental improvements to business, as well as systems, performance.

a. Rob Dearborn et al., *The Costs of Enterprise Downtime: North America 2004* (San Jose, CA: Infonetics Research, 2004), www.logicomputer.com/ pdf/downtime.pdf.

- How did the new technology reduce lights-on costs and help manage risks?

By following the principles discussed in the previous chapters, you have addressed the first three enterprise interests. Your new technology supports the IT-enabled business strategy, is generating benefits that exceed the one-time and ongoing costs, was delivered quickly with quality, and is being embraced and exploited by the end users.

So far, we haven't reviewed what you can do to help reduce lights-on costs and manage risks. Before we dive into this, let's take a moment to review why it's important.

Why Are IT Costs and Risks a Big Deal?

In 2003, Nicholas Carr caused a kerfuffle by concluding that IT doesn't provide sustainable competitive advantage, and, given that businesses are highly dependent on technology, the key to IT success is to "manage costs and risks meticulously."[4] In his carefully considered thesis, Carr suggests that sustained competitive advantage is conferred only by scarcity and that the ubiquity of information technologies means that they are "becoming costs of doing business that must be paid by all but provide distinction to none."[5]

Although there is widespread disagreement with this core thesis (yes, IT is ubiquitous, but the skill to apply it to reshape the enterprise's capabilities most certainly is not), Carr is spot-on about the need to become much more disciplined in IT spending and in understanding and managing the inherent vulnerabilities of technology.

Where Does All the Money Go?

Ongoing lights-on costs constitute, on average, 71 percent of total spending on IT.[6] It's hard to believe, but only 29 cents of each IT dollar is available to fund innovation, because the technology that has been acquired and developed over the past twenty to thirty years imposes a virtual 70 percent tax.

KTLO expenses are driven by a number of factors. Every dollar spent on new technology increases KTLO, because the technology must be operated, supported, and maintained. In addition, even though technology costs historically have declined, other costs have increased, such as:

- **Power:** As illustrated by a CIO who said, "I can no longer supply enough power to, or exhaust heat from, our datacenter. I feel like I'm running hot plates, not computers."[7]

- **Data storage:** Demand is "rising nearly 80 percent a year worldwide" and storage costs make up, "on average, between 30 percent and 50 percent of a company's IT budget."[8]

- **Regulatory compliance:** Research indicates that IT spends as much as 15 percent of its budget on financial compliance.[9]

It takes more money each year to feed the KTLO beast. But with constant vigilance it's possible to reduce KTLO to 50 percent.[10] To starve the beast (or at least put it on a diet), IT organizations are working hard to decompose KTLO costs into services (which business partners "buy," even if they don't actually pay for them), consumption levels, and cost per unit.[11] With this information in hand, IT leaders can identify efficiency opportunities (reducing cost per unit) and work with their business partners on lowering consumption (by, for example, training their staffs, using self-service features, eliminating duplicate systems, accepting lower service levels, etc.).

Unfortunately, the decomposition of KTLO is a work in progress, putting CIOs in a world of hurt at budget time because they find it difficult to back up their projections. As a result, KTLO is often underfunded, leading to a deterioration in technology performance that impacts business productivity in subtle ways because the cause and effect are difficult to trace and manage. And, because calls need to be answered, transactions need to be processed, broken systems need to be repaired, and changing regulations need to be addressed, IT often taps in to project funds to supplement underfunded KTLO budgets, impacting innovation funding even further.

IT-smart business leaders understand the impact of this KTLO funding dance of doom, causing business leaders to state, "I wish we could consistently support the new technology that we build. The company will make the investments and we ask for the operating expense to support it, but we never get enough funding for what is built."[12] These leaders wisely observe that "hoping that things don't break isn't a strategy."[13]

The overall goal is to reduce KTLO expenses year over year as a percentage of revenue in order to increase the capacity for innovation (to fund strategic and enhancement initiatives). This objective isn't easy to attain, because IT costs have been under tight scrutiny in response to runaway spending in the late 1990s and the financial crisis that hit in 2008. As a result, much of the low-hanging fruit, such as consolidating data centers and call centers, renegotiating contracts, and offshoring IT services, has been picked and eaten.

Further KTLO saving needs to come from standardizing and simplifying existing applications and infrastructure technology. Because each change migrated to production carries with it the potential to mess up or clean up the existing technology, achieving further KTLO reductions requires an even closer partnership among and IT and its business counterparts.

What Is IT Doing to Reduce KTLO?

IT is working hard to drive down KTLO costs by retiring and modernizing technology, reducing consumption, increasing utilization, delaying purchases, streamlining processes, and automating manual activities:

- **Retiring, consolidating, and modernizing technology:** Retiring underutilized technologies and consolidating and modernizing technologies has been shown to reduce overall KTLO expense between 10 and 20 percent.

- **Reducing consumption:** Defining usage policies (e.g., music downloads, Web radio usage, e-mail inbox and attachment limits, file retention, etc.) helps reduce consumption of computing, network, and storage resources.

- **Increasing utilization:** Utilization can be increased through sharing computing and storage resources. (The average Windows server runs at "8 percent to 12 percent [of] capacity," and "most enterprises use only 30–45 percent of the storage they have allocated.")[14]

- **Delaying purchases:** Technology purchases can be delayed by upgrading existing technology (e.g., memory upgrades, data storage, etc.) and redeploying older technology to support lighter needs.

- **Streamlining processes:** Implementing disciplined IT service management processes can result in an efficiency gain of as much as 40 percent.[15]

- **Automating manual activities:** Once processes are streamlined, introducing automation tools can significantly reduce staffing (e.g., monitoring and management tools can increase the number of servers administrators can manage by tenfold).

What Can I Do to Lower KTLO?

To support a minimalist, simplified, standardized approach to IT, focus your customization requirements on necessary, versus unnecessary, differences.

- **Focus on the functionality that drives your business case and not the technology that delivers the functionality:** Ask IT to generate multiple alternatives (leverage existing systems versus buy versus build) and to include the KTLO costs (also called total costs of ownership) when comparing the returns.

- **Focus on the extent to which the functionality is used and not the amount of functionality delivered:** When you scope technology, focus on the features that drive the targeted benefits. When you implement packaged software, minimize changes to non-differentiating processes. When you deploy technology, hold your people accountable for understanding and using it properly. Improper use can drive up IT's support requirements significantly, as illustrated by this example shared by an IT support leader: "Seventy-five percent of the issues that were escalated to the ERP team were actually problems with the way the end users entered the data."[16]

- **Focus on buying technology that is well built, and don't buy technology only because it is already built or cheaper to build:** Ask IT how the design of the new technology will leverage or reuse existing systems, comply with technology standards, and clean up duplicated systems, inconsistent data, and complicated interfaces. Don't get lulled into buying technology from external providers without understanding how well it will play with what's in place and what's planned.

- **Focus on the service levels delivered and not on who is delivering the services:** When defining service levels, ask for only what you need to support your business (e.g., weekend support for HR processes is usually not necessary), and help IT obtain the necessary funds. Hold your people accountable for fully exploiting the configuration features that allow them to change the technology without support from IT (e.g., many software packages are delivered with easy-to-use tools that allow changes to screen layouts, process flows, business rules, data extracts, and reporting). Encourage your people to manage their passwords (password management can account for as many as 30 percent of help desk calls), and use self-service tools (the average help desk call costs $27.60—twice the cost of self-service options).[17]

Lowering KTLO requires constant vigilance and is difficult because it requires working all these opportunities simultaneously. As Randy Mott, CIO of Hewlett-Packard, said, "Trying to pick and choose among various and equally pressing IT priorities—server consolidation, application portfolio management, rationalizing IT resources—is a recipe for failure. Choosing is losing."[18]

What Can I Do to Manage Risks?

Imagine this. Bad luck just seems to follow you around. First your dog was run over, then your priceless Monet was stolen from your front steps, and now, your house is flooded because of a botched-up repair to the water heater. You reported the incidents to the police, who promptly came to your aid and assisted in the disposal of your dog, completion of a stolen property report, and submittal of an insurance claim. Sure, they were polite enough, but they didn't seem to accept responsibility. In fact, they seemed to imply that you need to be more careful with your house and home.

Although this scenario is extreme, this attitude leads many business leaders to ignore their own responsibility for ensuring smooth business operations by protecting the integrity of their technology and information. In a recent survey, more than one-half of business leaders responded that "deciding how much security and privacy risk is acceptable" is "more or completely IT's responsibility."[19]

This means that more than one-half of business leaders are clueless about IT risk management. IT risk is business risk, because technology failures can crater the supply chain, expose sensitive data to unauthorized access, and result in bad decisions due to bad data—causing customers to defect, regulators to lose faith, and productivity to decline. IT risk management is becoming more critical and complex with each passing day, given the perfect storm of expanded regulatory oversight, increased technology dependence, and emerging anytime-anywhere business models.[20]

Just as you wouldn't expect the police to protect your wandering dog, leaders in charge of order processing teams, sales forces, and distribution centers shouldn't defer their security responsibilities to their company's chief security officer, chief information officer, or risk management board. Instead, on a day-in, day-out basis, work with IT to protect the systems and information that support your business so that business as usual is, well, usual. Arrange for your relationship manager to introduce you to the IT risk management wonks so that you can understand the following:

- Who governs enterprise and IT risk management and which controls and policies have been defined

- Which controls and policies pertain to your operational responsibilities so that you can help ensure availability (keeping existing processes running and recovering from interruption), accessibility (ensuring that only authorized people have access to information and facilities), accuracy (providing timely, accurate, and complete data), and agility (quickly implementing new strategic initiatives)[21]

- How to educate your people and modify processes to support the controls and policies

- What information is available to monitor compliance and how to be sure you are notified of necessary changes in policies and controls

Risk management is not about eliminating risks but about being aware of risks so that you can determine the right level of risk to assume and how to mitigate risk to close the gap between where you are and where you want to be. As you work through this process, make sure you can answer the questions listed in table 6-1.

If you are dogged (pun intended) in your pursuit of getting these questions addressed, you will have a big impact on protecting your business. In addition, reducing KTLO expenses (through standardization and simplification) also reduces risk

TABLE 6-1

Risk management objectives

To manage your technology risk	A few scary facts
1. Available	
If performance starts to degrade, are you notified? If your systems die, can you get them up quickly? If your facility or data center were destroyed, could you still run your business?	System downtime or degradation extracts up to 3.6% of revenue.[a] "Most organizations think they have a disaster recovery plan in place, only to find out it's inadequate."[b]
2. Accessible	
Are there intrusion prevention and detection controls in place? Do you have control over who accesses your systems or data? Do you test and approve changes to your systems or data?	"70% of security incidents that occur . . . are inside jobs, making the insider threat arguably the most critical one facing the enterprise."[c]
3. Accurate	
Do your systems and data effectively support your business processes? Are you notified if activity and data are out of expected ranges? Are you in compliance with regulations?	"There is not a company on the planet that does not have a data problem."[d]
4. Agile	
Can your systems be modified easily to meet new business requirements?	Nearly two-thirds of C-level executives "say their organizations are at risk from information- and technology-based disruption."[e]

a. "The Costs of Enterprise Downtime, North America 2004," Infonetics Research, February 2004, www.logicomputer.com/pdf/downtime.pdf.

b. Dan Tynan, "Seven Things IT Should Be Doing (but Isn't)," *Infoworld,* July 21, 2008.

c. Chad Dickerson, "Top 20 IT Mistakes to Avoid," *Infoworld,* November 19, 2004.

d. Colin Barker, "Gartner: It's Business Intelligence 2.0 Time," ZDNet Asia, January 2007, http://www.zdnetasia.com/news/business/0,39044229,61985906,00.htm.

e. Business Technology Office, "IT's Unmet Potential: McKinsey Global Survey Results," *McKinsey Quarterly,* December 2008, 2.

exposure and vice versa. Technology consolidation, standardization, automation, and process discipline are central to effective risk management programs, and, according to Karen Kotowski, CIO of Sallie Mae, "companies that correct their underlying data and systems improve their overall efficiency since exceptions are minimized."[22] Do what you can, where you can, to secure your business by working with IT to implement your own technologically savvy version of community-based policing and a neighborhood watch program.

What's the New Partnership?

The ongoing operational costs of new technology exceed the initial development costs by a significant factor. Traditionally, business leaders have focused on obtaining funds for new development, with little concern about how alternative approaches to designing and supporting the technology would impact KTLO costs. Help IT help you by focusing customizations on necessary differences—those requirements that impact functionality, integration, service levels, and returns—and keeping everything else as standard and simple as possible.

Expect IT leaders to help you help them by driving down year-over-year KTLO expenses, defining target architectures and renewal plans, and implementing service catalogs and management processes that make it easy to understand and request IT products and services and help ensure consistent, predictable delivery.

7

You Need Innovation, and IT Functions in Bureaucracy

I've got a great idea!

I've got amazing bureaucracy!

At this point, you might be wondering whether the paradoxical secret to innovation is bureaucracy.[1] Strategy making, demand management, project management, service management—it's enough to make your head explode. Some 37 percent of IT leaders and more than 50 percent of business leaders agree with the statement, "IT is overly bureaucratic and control oriented."[2]

IT is frequently perceived as "not being the technology innovator in their company, but rather the dead weight keeping the real technology innovators—employees who want to use the tools . . . from taking matters in their own hands."[3] Many leaders want to know why, given the rapid pace of technology innovation, innovating with technology is a slow and painful process.

By their nature, technologists want nothing more than for you to say, "Wow, how did you do that?" rather than, "Gee, why can't you do that?" But on a day-in, day-out basis, they are overwhelmed with requests they struggle to fulfill given the complexity of the installed technologies, the need to promote enterprise interests, and the lack of resources available to support the enterprise and the people within it.

- **Existing IT complexity:** The approach of building "point," or one-time, solutions to respond quickly to business needs has led, over time, to the opposite result. About 61 percent of companies operate on a mishmash of technology that is difficult to understand and change and expensive to operate. One-fourth of companies haven't yet started on the journey to standardize and consolidate technologies, and an additional 36 percent are just starting the process of introducing IT standards to reduce costs, risks, and development cycle time.[4]

- **Promote enterprise interests:** Once companies commit to standardizing technology, competitive realities dictate that they focus on reducing costs and improving customer service by implementing an enterprise-wide operating model consisting of business processes supported by information management capabilities that provide consistent, timely, and accurate information. Once this is in place, innovation increases as the assets are reused to extend the business model.[5] To implement an enterprise-wide operating model, decision authorities must shift from functional and divisional business leaders to the enterprise. This practice has the unfortunate effect of reducing localized authority and funding—and consequently innovation. In the quest to implement common processes, the enterprise technology mantra becomes, "You get what you get and you don't throw a fit." Although this approach works well to clean up issues from years of decentralized and uncoordinated decision making, it frustrates individuals and small teams that are fueled to innovate but are stymied in their ability to do so.

- **Lack of resources:** IT doesn't have the resource capacity to proactively support the organization and the individual needs of the people within it. What IT professional in her right mind has the time or inclination to go out looking for what might be when it's hard enough dealing with what is? Yet this is exactly what business leaders want their IT organizations to do. They want IT to show them how to exploit the current tools and discuss future possibilities about how IT can be used to drive the business. This never gets to the top of IT's priority list. It's true that IT studies current practices and redesigns work flows pertaining to funded initiatives, but on an ongoing basis, IT rarely studies how systems are being used and the unintended uses of the installed technologies. Every organization has internal and external *lead users* who, by their very nature, innovate on a daily basis.[6] These innovators "can develop exactly what they want, rather than relying on manufacturers to act as their (often very imperfect) agents."[7] Like the proverbial tree in the forest, are lead users really innovating if no one's watching? For if no one is watching, then

the innovations remain the domain of the inventor—
potentially of value but practically invisible to the rest of
the organization. Lead user employees are innovating in
relative anonymity because their leaders are looking out
and up, not down; thinking about tomorrow, not today;
thinking big, not little. The same goes for IT. IT is focused
on managing demand from above and not on creating it
from below.

Do you recall *Winnie the Pooh*? When it comes to innovation,
IT behaves like Eeyore to the Tigger-like innovators. Like the
always negative Eeyore, IT professionals *can't* (make quick
changes to the complex technology), *don't want to* (implement
solutions that don't support enterprise-wide interests), and *don't
have time* (to support localized innovation by working with lead
users.)

Why Can't We Outsource IT?

It would be great to outsource this big old hairy problem, but it's
a bad idea. IT isn't an organizational structure, it's an organizational asset, and companies need to ensure that leaders at all levels have a permanent sense of responsibility for managing IT.
Research on IT management practices within the banking industry, for example, found that top-performing companies outsource less, and those that outsource IT on a wholesale basis
"struggle to use IT to drive value and have limited strategic flexibility as the business context evolves and hardware prices plum-
met."[8] Outsourcing makes sense to access specialized expertise,
flexible supply, and cheaper services (made possible through
economies of scale). But "IT costs and services are not likely to

improve significantly with outsourcing until business people change their habits."[9]

Senior executives need to focus relentlessly on defining the company's target operating model and ensure that the necessary capabilities are encoded within a digitized platform to be leveraged for profitable growth. Leaders at *every* level need to assume more accountability for the IT assets that fuel their business by elevating the relationship with IT, innovating through experimentation, and getting smarter about IT.

Assume Accountability

In general, business leaders are too passive when it comes to management of the IT asset. By their own admission, only 25 percent of business leaders manage IT-enabled initiatives and drive IT-enabled business change, with the reminder relying on IT to lead the charge.[10] As observed by a seasoned IT leader who recently moved into "the business," "The business view of IT is worse than I thought. The current relationship is similar to one that you have with a mechanic when you know nothing about cars. The business leaders hold their cards close to their vest, trying to evoke the right behavior from IT, and often the wrong thing or nothing is delivered because we have the wrong conversations."[11]

If you haven't done so already, give up the fantasy that IT is going to innovate for you. IT can play a big role in enabling innovation, but if you aren't innovating, IT can't help you. Even if IT had all day, every day, to think about how to reshape your business, it can't do so alone.

Reading the techno tea leaves, with any level of accuracy, requires nurturing and learning from lead users. As one expert said, "Product developers need two types of information to succeed at their work: need and context-of-use information generated by users and generic solution information [possessed by IT]."[12] It's not easy for users or IT professionals to communicate their respective needs to each other. Requirements documents go only so far. Innovation requires hands-on work and real-time IT–business collaboration to discover how people do their work, explore proposed process changes and new ways to analyze the business, create and validate visual prototypes, and conduct pilots.

Elevate Your Relationship with IT

It's impossible to innovate without help from IT, for it holds the keys to the IT kingdom. Elevate your relationship with IT by no longer asking IT to support things that you can do for yourself. In return, ask IT to create an IT "gifted and talented" program ("IT Gate") that gives lead users special IT privileges—the best tools, equipment, education, and support—as long as they agree to "first do no harm," clean up their own messes, and support the less talented around them. Your lead users (or power users) are the ones who drive IT crazy. These users want more, they want it all, and they want it now.

Have your lead users support your "barely users" by creating a no user left behind program. In return for IT Gate status, lead users should provide just-in-time education and support to increase the adoption of technologies in place, diagnose problems before they are reported to IT, and prioritize or handle the enhancement requests (using, for example, ERP software configuration tools). Over time, improved education and accountability will reduce these support requirements, freeing up lead users and IT to do more innovating and less remedial support.

Although this "you do this, I'll do that" exchange sounds like a win-win, be prepared for some resistance from IT, trust your instincts, and be ready to spend some money.

- **Be prepared for resistance:** There are some crusty dogs in IT who don't believe that their business counterparts can do more for themselves without getting into trouble. In the words of one CIO, "My staff was convinced that they'd write bad queries that would lead to bad decision making . . . and bring down our environments. But . . . a funny thing starts to happen when you sit side by side with a person for a few weeks. You build a relationship. You build trust. You celebrate when they master a concept. Then the light goes off in IT that they might actually be able to do this, and this work that I hate (ad hoc queries, custom reports, etc.) might actually diminish."[13]

- **Trust your instincts:** If something looks wrong, it probably is wrong. In the words of one senior IT leader, "If you have a crazy process that takes five people and it feels like it should take two, or if your people have to navigate six screens to do one task, it's a problem. Keep a running list, and challenge your lead users and IT as to what is going to be done and when."[14] Be sure to ask for alternatives (small, medium, and large), and if the recommended solution is out of proportion to the benefits, ask for a second opinion and go outside to get one if need be.

- **Open your wallet:** The money center is the power center, and if you're willing to pay the bills, it will open some doors—as long as you do it with IT's blessing. But before you spend a dime, find out what's been budgeted and who holds approval over the funds. IT-smart companies put the "enhancement" portion of the portfolio into the hands of the business leaders (by creating business unit governance over IT checkbooks and defining policies governing its use).

The fundamental principle in elevating the relationship with IT is to give lead users more of what they want by freeing up a good chunk of IT's time to support and study what these users are doing (and why) so that the most promising innovations can be standardized and scaled to benefit the enterprise. By their nature, lead users and technologists love to innovate. They don't need to be assigned to a task force, paid more money, or even given special recognition. They innovate because that's who they are. Find them. Connect with them. Nurture them. Benefit from them.

Run Experiments, Not Projects

Recently, I asked some business leaders for their top three IT wishes. Across the board, their responses echoed a common plea: "I wish IT projects would come in on time and on budget." The funny thing is, this reasonable-sounding request is actually quite unreasonable. We are no longer simply automating existing manual processes. We are trying to change the way people think and behave. Who really knows what's going to happen when:

- Field agents are given access to real-time business information?

- High-priced consultants are given a virtual workspace that consists of instant messaging, telephony, and audio- and videoconferencing as well as real-time document sharing, virtual whiteboards, and PC-to-PC audio- and videoconferencing?

- Franchisees are given a Web-based system to quickly source parts needed by their customers from any major manufacturer?

Innovative applications of information technology begin with someone asking, "What if?" Innovative people and teams guess or hypothesize how new capabilities will change behavior. Hypotheses are tested via experiments. Although the inputs to the experiments are known (in terms of the approach and resources necessary to figure out whether A+B impacts Z), the outcome of experiments, by definition, is unknown and more often than not will be along the lines of, "Back to the drawing board."

To obtain resources for IT-enabled experimentation, business leaders must invent a business case that sounds deterministic, and not probabilistic, in terms of outcomes. The experiment becomes a project, and, in this transformation, expectations shift to assume that there are many more knowns than unknowns. The false assumption of precision—that when we do A+B, the outcome will be Z—is used to drive the project plan and functional requirements.

In the course of the project, in the quest to deliver Z, business leaders are forced to perform experiments. This practice frustrates IT to no end. As the project goes through multiple iterations of replacing A with C and adding D, in order to get the desired outcome, scope changes and the project costs and time lines escalate. The inability to deliver against time, budget, and scope is disheartening for everyone and, left unchecked, will eventually inhibit innovation. Business leaders are less likely to ask the "What if?" questions. IT learns to pad its budgets and time lines to the point of killing ideas at birth. The IT investment council becomes jaded about IT-enabled investments and asks for additional justification, thus reinforcing the negative cycle.

There is a better way. Once we accept that projects are really a series of experiments, we can approach them accordingly:

- Prepare a business case, and estimate overall funding needs based on a sequential plan of experiments.

- Request funding for the first experiment, and define success as the ability to prove or disprove a hypothesis (e.g., franchisees will use an online tool provided that it has the following information and performance) or gain additional information (e.g., this is the information that the agents want).

- At the end of each experiment, determine what was learned and revise the business case and the sequential plan of experiments. Request funding for the next experiment provided that the overall business case still makes sense.

This approach works great for business leaders who are able to verify the impact of their experiments and is resisted by those unable to do so. This is because IT investment boards often take a portfolio approach to funding experiments (as if they were venture capitalists) and wisely prune experiments that aren't proving out, shifting these monies to fund new experiments or scale existing ones.

Keep in mind that the working prototype or cobbled-together pilot system developed in support of the experiment will need to be redesigned to address enterprise needs for scalability, reliability, standardization, and integration. Redeveloping the prototype or pilot isn't a waste of time or money but a reality of technology innovation, as observed by many over the years:

> *"Technology is a word that describes something that doesn't work yet."*[15]

> *"Experience is something you don't get until just after you need it."*[16]

> *"Systems are like pancakes and babies—throw the first one away."*[17]

To plan for this eventuality, include rebuilding costs in the business case. Doing so will encourage IT and your people to use the cheapest means possible to prove the viability of a concept without being saddled with trying to make the system industrial strength during the experimentation process.

Invest in IT Smarts

Overall, business leaders don't feel very smart about IT. For example, in a recent survey only one-fourth reported that they are IT-smart, and about half admit that they:

- Make half-baked requests

- Want it all, regardless of ROI

- Change their minds about what they want their systems to do

- Don't know how to use the systems in place[18]

This lack of IT competence and confidence means that the IT bureaucracy will chew them up and spit them out. Ensure that you have at least one person on your team who is a lead or power user, because, from an IT point of view, "business groups who have somebody on their team who is an IT expert do much better with IT [in leveraging technology to meet their needs] than those who do not."[19] If you are lucky enough to have an IT relationship manager or analyst supporting your group, treat him like a full-fledged team member (give him office space and include him in all the staff meetings, off-sites, team builds, etc.) so that he starts wearing your team uniform. Technologists take enormous pride in seeing the impact of their work on the business, so do everything you can do include them as you plan, play, and celebrate the game.

Make sure that you and your people have access to (and mastery of) the technology tools necessary to run your business and experiment with new ways to work. A recent survey on enterprise systems reported that "most organizations use only 64 percent of their enterprise systems' core functions," with 20 percent of the respondents explaining that "they didn't make use of all the functionality due to lack of time to learn how to apply them."[20] This isn't about doing IT's job; it's about giving your people the capability to discover value-added opportunities and develop visual requirements to facilitate productive communication with IT. The difficulty that users have in communicating their *context of use* requirements—what their job entails and how they do it and would like to do it—can be resolved by giving lead users *innovation toolkits,* allowing IT to study what lead users create and understand how to exploit these ideas on a broader basis.[21]

Excel is a great example of an innovation toolkit. The compliance wonks may hate spreadsheets, but, without a doubt, Excel has played an important role as an innovation tool. Many an organization would be better off had it devoted resources to examine how Excel was being used and standardizing and scaling the resulting innovations rather than trying to mandate out-of-context tools defined from above or acquired from outside.

If you're wondering what an innovation toolkit should consist of, ask your lead users and IT which tools they use and which ones they want. At minimum, your people should understand the applications, data repositories, reporting, data query and analysis, and end user productivity tools in place that relate to the business processes they support. Productivity tools that facilitate innovation include the following.

- **Presentations:** For shaping and storyboarding ideas

- **Spreadsheets:** For analyzing data, reporting, and proving out data models, calculations, and reports

- **Data analysis and reporting:** For advanced data extracting, manipulating, and reporting

- **Work flow and diagramming:** For designing new work flows and data models

- **Content management:** For designing and sharing new forms and documents

- **Web publishing and collaboration:** For sharing ideas and innovations

Encourage innovation by sharing what's going on across the company and in competitor and analogous companies, asking "What if?" questions, and celebrating both progress and "good tries." Take the advice of an IT-savvy lead user: work out a deal with IT to provide a person to be "on call for the innovators, as good ideas can get derailed simply because the proper IT resources aren't there to get things out of the mud," and establish a "safe haven network where users feel free to try anything within the bounds of the innovation rules without fearing harm to the network or disrupting core business."[22]

Remember—the simpler, the better. A few tools in competent, motivated hands with active support from leadership and IT are all that lead users need to do what they do best.

What About Technology?

For an IT book, this one has very little discussion of technology—and for good reason. Good technology leadership transcends technology. As the old saying goes, "A fool with a tool is still a fool." Technology's not magic, but "business leaders seem to think that, if they only had the right technology, their business life would be easier."[23] Technology, as you know, doesn't make things easier; it takes a lot of work to make technology work. The beliefs that "more is better" and "it's going to be easier" set the stage for overly complex products (which remain largely unused) and disappointment. That being said, as an innovator, you need to understand the emerging technologies that are impacting our companies, our work, and our lives. To help you get started, a summary of trends and emerging technologies is included in appendix B.

What's the New Partnership?

Many people ask, "Why, given the rapid pace of technology innovation, is innovating with technology such a slow and painful process?" The answer? "Love the people. Hate the system."

It's OK to hate the system. IT hates it, too. Just as you don't get frustrated when HR won't let you hire or fire on a whim or when finance doesn't let you blow your budget without approval, there's no reason to be frustrated with the people in IT. Instead, help IT help you by developing IT smarts, holding your team members accountable for fully exploiting their tools, and elevating the relationship with IT so that it can support your innovation efforts. In turn, expect IT leaders to help you help them by providing education, fostering IT self-sufficiency, and creating an IT gifted and talented program.

By committing to forge a new partnership, business and IT leaders will move beyond the frustrations and help each other fully exploit IT to the benefit of the enterprise and the people within it. Table 7-1 summarizes the fundamental leadership principles of the new partnership.

TABLE 7-1

Leadership principles of the new partnership

Helping IT help the business	Helping the business help IT
• Embrace enterprise interests.	• Clarify and streamline decision making.
• Strengthen relationships with IT.	• Create a business-savvy and service-oriented IT organization.
• Develop IT-enabled business strategies.	• Facilitate the development of IT-enabled business strategies and enterprise architectures.
• Generate value from IT-enabled investments.	
• Deliver quickly and with quality.	• Ensure that IT-enabled value is realized.
• Focus customizations on necessary differences.	• Deliver quickly and with quality.
• Invest in IT smarts.	• Drive down year-over-year lights-on expenses.
• Assume permanent accountability for the IT assets that fuel your business.	• Enhance business partner self-sufficiency.
	• Fully democratize IT.

A detailed list of the responsibilities of the new partnership is included in appendix C. Before you read chapter 8, take some time to review the appendix and identify opportunities for improvement. Then proceed to chapter 8 to turn your insights into action.

8

You Need Good IT, and IT Can Become Great

Hey, our IT is pretty good!

Yes, but it's not great...

Every company has the IT capability it deserves. If you've decided that your organization deserves better, it's time to decide what you're going to do about it. It's my hope that this book has changed how you view IT, convinced you that managing the IT asset is part of your real job, and given you the knowledge to move past the frustrations and form a new partnership with IT.

Toward that end, imagine that you're on a plane, having just finished this book. You want to share what you've learned with your team, and you decide to draft an e-mail about the key concepts and implications going forward. First you summarize what you've learned:

Our company's ability to thrive in the "connect and collaborate" future depends on IT-smart business leaders and business-smart IT leaders who understand how to work together. Companies that are smart about managing IT outperform those that aren't. Underperforming companies make bad investments, ignore the inherent risks of developing and deploying technology, and spend too much money operating fragmented systems on "technology du jour" infrastructures using informal, undocumented processes. For these underperformers, there is no correlation between IT spending and financial outcomes.

Next, you reflect on the state of IT management at your company.

We treat IT as some sort of servant-genie—expecting to get our wishes granted—and we're frustrated when the genie asks for information and resources and impinges on our "real work." If I'm being honest, line managers have responded to IT's pleas for increased engagement with passive-aggressive behavior. We assign junior resources and treat project sponsorship as a temporary, ceremonial job that consists primarily of showing up at IT steering committee meetings.

Then you move to recommendations on how to improve IT management practices.

From now on, we need a closer partnership with IT across the entire value chain of IT planning, investing, innovating, delivering, and operating. We need to work with IT to create IT-smart business leaders and business-smart IT leaders, in support of the four enterprise interests: first, how do we increase the value realized from our IT investments? Second, how do we improve the success of our projects and change initiatives? Third, how do we ensure coherent architectures to enable horizontal integration, flexibility, and agility? Fourth, how do we reduce our lights-on costs to increase innovation capacity and appropriately manage risks?

You want to close the e-mail with specific commitments but aren't sure what to write. You try to channel your inner Gandhi and "be the change you want the world to be," but you're stuck. How can a mid-level business leader, like you, begin to make a difference? Shifting in your coach seat, you see someone across the aisle reading the book *Good to Great*, and it hits you: "My team needs to meet with our IT partners to confront the brutal facts about how well we're supporting the four enterprise interests. Based on the results of these discussions, we can work together and outline an approach to better manage the IT asset."

OK, I just put words in your mouth, but now it's your turn. Bring out a sheet of paper and take a moment to answer these questions for yourself:

- What have I learned?

_____

_____

_____

_____

_____

_____

• What frustrates me about IT?

_____

_____

_____

_____

• How I am contributing to my frustrations with IT?

_____

_____

_____

_____

• What am I going to do about IT?

_____

_____

_____

_____

Hopefully, one thing you're going to "do about IT" is to get to-gether with your team and confront the brutal facts. Toward that end, use the worksheet in figure 8-1 to help guide this discussion (you can download a soft copy from www.8hates.com). Complete

FIGURE 8-1

How well are we managing the IT asset?

Enterprise IT interests	Supporting behaviors	Current performance? Good/Average/ Poor	Relative impact? High/ Med/Low
How do we increase the value realized from our IT investments?	• Is business and IT strategy developed concurrently? • Are business leaders held accountable for value realization? • Are system capabilities used, and are key systems available as needed? • Are business and IT partners increasingly satisfied with the level of collaboration and delivery?		
How do we improve the success of projects and change initiatives?	• Does the prioritization process assess relative value, urgency, affordability, and commitment? • Is project success defined and measured, and are the measures used to manage scope and ascertain progress? • Are projects (along with funding) time-boxed to deliver value every 3–6 months, and are kill switches used to ensure that underperforming projects "fail fast"? • Is IT held accountable for delivering on time and on budget?		
How do we ensure coherent architectures to enable flexibility and agility?	• Has the company identified the operating model and the "to be" and "as is" architectures for business processes, information, applications, and technologies? • Is off-the-shelf, on-demand (vs. built-to-order) infrastructure capacity available?		

(Continued)

145

FIGURE 8-1 (continued)

How well are we managing the IT asset?

Enterprise IT interests	Supporting behaviors	Current performance? Good/Average/ Poor	Relative impact? High/ Med/Low
How do we reduce our lights-on costs to increase innovation capacity and manage risks?	• Are lights-on costs decreasing as a percent of revenue? • Is IT delivering on service level agreements? • Are the installed technologies and applications suitable for their purpose? • Are technology and process standards used to promote consolidation, automation, and reuse? • Is the enterprise in compliance, and are availability, accessibility, accuracy, and agility risks known and managed?		

this form together, and then brainstorm how to address the low-performing, high-impact behaviors.

Although you are committed to being the change you want the world to be, if you're like most leaders, you already think you are the change. Most of us think we are better than we really are; for example, "94 percent of men rank themselves in the top half according to male athletic ability."[1] Get a grip on reality by soliciting confidential feedback from your counterparts in IT. And while you're at it, do the same for them—and then compare results (to make it easy, you can use the "How IT-Smart Are Our Organizations?" survey available at www.8hates.com).

Feedback is useless unless you understand it, own it, and act on it. Comparing respective views is uncomfortable, but it's no more uncomfortable than perpetuating a mutually frustrating relationship in which everything's too little, too late, and too expensive. Write down your insights and commitments, and ask your IT counterparts to do the same. Document what is going to be done and by what date, and hold each other accountable.

Asking and responding to feedback will help strengthen your relationship with your IT counterparts, because it demonstrates that you respect their point of view, trust them to tell you the truth, and are committed to working together to do great things. It will also increase the likelihood that they will change in reaction to the changes you make.

Why Does Every Company Have the IT Capability It Deserves?

By default or design, companies have the IT capability they've bought and paid for. Don't believe me? Check out the CIO. Chances are, if you wouldn't want to have lunch with her, then the powers that be at the top of your organization either don't know what they want from IT or prefer that IT play in the background, not the foreground.

The CIO, and the IT organization as a whole, reflects an organization's understanding and aspirations for IT. To understand what your organization wants IT to do, identify the role that best describes your IT organizational capability.[2]

- **The "butler."** This is the concierge view of IT. In these organizations IT is expected to play a supporting role, responding to and fulfilling requests from the business in a "no fuss, no muss" manner. Although this may sound like heaven on earth, understand that butler IT organizations will not innovate or lead in technology application or adoption. In partnering, the best you can expect is a professional service provider and not a strategic partner.

- **The "grinder."** This is the commodity view of IT. In these organizations IT is expected to play a tactical role, providing basic IT services at low cost. In focusing primarily on efficiency, this organization will not be able to develop strong business partnerships, deliver top-notch services, and apply technology to drive shareholder value.

- **The "team player."** This is the operational support view of IT. In this organization IT is expected to run efficiently and work collaboratively with its business partners to embed technology in business processes. IT is considered central to operating the business efficiently and reducing the costs and risk of operations, but it is totally dependent on business partners for their insights about applying technology for competitive differentiation.

- **The "entrepreneur."** This is the innovative IT organization. In this organization IT is expected to lead the business in applying technology to improve the company's strategic differentiation. IT governance is baked in to overall corporate governance, and the CIO reports to the highest levels of the organization, frequently discussing key issues with the board of directors.

Whether your IT baby is smart or dumb—or somewhere in between—understand that the current state reflects many years of (conscious or unconscious) senior leadership parenting.

What If My IT Is Really, Really Bad?

There are two major reasons an IT organization is "bad," and what you do about it differs depending on the root cause.

- **Mismatch between your expectations and the role.** If your current IT capability reflects the grinder but you need a team player, don't blame IT. As an analogy, you don't hire an auditor to do financial planning and then pick on her when she doesn't do a good job. If expectations are mismatched, you can make the best of what you have (e.g., live with a subpar financial plan) or serve yourself (e.g., develop your own financial plan or hire someone qualified to get it done). If you decide to serve yourself, understand that you won't get accolades for your extra work, because the powers that be don't know what they are missing (i.e., they don't know why a financial plan is necessary).

- **Inability to fully deliver on the role.** If the role matches your needs but IT isn't delivering, then determine whether the poor performance is a result of organizational maturity or leadership. If you have a strong CIO and IT leadership team in place and they're working hard to retool the organization to fulfill expectations, then give them a break and a helping hand. If you have an IT leadership team that is clueless about its lack of delivery, you have no choice except to do without or serve yourself.

If you decide to serve yourself, make sure that you follow these steps.

1. Hire a really good IT person to work on your team but reside with IT (so that you don't get accused of creating a shadow IT organization).

2. Incorporate IT smarts into the hiring criteria and development plans of your team members.

3. Collaborate so well that IT trusts you to act independently, confident that you will keep it informed, follow the rules, and share the credit.

4. Develop partnerships with external IT service providers to help you do whatever your internal IT group cannot (make strategy, innovate, deliver, operate). There's a whole world of virtual IT resources waiting to take care of you. Just make sure you invite IT to go along for the ride.

There is one other option. If you're mad as hell and not going to take it anymore, why don't you raise your hand and offer to move into IT and fix things? This works, of course, only if you have a senior-level sponsor or are willing to sacrifice your career. Moving into IT is seen, in many organizations, as a one-way street.

Is This as Good as IT Gets?

Nope. Even if you follow through and implement all these recommendations and transform yourself into the very model of a modern IT business leader, the result will be good—but not great—IT. Why bother? It's for one crucial reason: creating IT-smart business leaders is a prerequisite to fully democratizing innovation. And, once innovation is democratized, your organization's IT capability will finally move from good to great.

To review the difference between good and great IT, let's review the IT operating principles of the company, NetApp, as shown in table 8-1.[3]

Although this is good, it isn't nearly as good as IT can get. That's because "good IT" is based on the assumption that IT

TABLE 8-1

NetApp: An illustration of good IT operating principles

Enterprise interest	Operating principles
Increase value realized from IT.	Top line, bottom line, and customer focused: "Any system that allows us to get closer to our customers and partners." Business leaders held accountable for realizing value: "Business to justify its IT investments and to present a tangible return on investment for all projects."
Improve success of projects and change initiatives.	Fast-cycle delivery: "Deliver tangible business value within 90-day increments."
Ensure coherent architectures to enable flexibility and agility.	Fast-cycle innovation tied to long-term interests: "Build quickly while also looking at least two or three years ahead."
Reduce lights-on costs and manage risks.	Business-smart IT and IT-smart business: "IT leaders who challenge [the business]" and "Each cross functional process has a sponsor at the senior or executive VP level . . . with operational leader whose responsibility includes that business process."

must provide all IT-related products and services. To do so, governance, like demand management, must stand between the requester and the provider, thus inhibiting innovation ("Folks in the lower levels of the organization occasionally criticize the process as painful and time consuming"[4]). Business leaders seeking approval and resources for IT-enabled initiatives and services are forced to wait in line for funding and resources before they can test and implement their great ideas, thus diminishing the organization's overall capacity to innovate.

The concepts outlined in this book can help organizations go from bad to good but not good to great, because they don't resolve the perennial IT challenge of how to fit a hundred pounds of demand into a twenty-five-pound bag. The future of IT depends on expanding supply to meet the demands of the business.

What Does Great IT Look Like?

The future of IT calls for fully democratizing IT-enabled innovation. To prevent anarchy, this idea requires a guided democracy consisting of lightweight governance supported by a digitized platform that ensures enterprise coherence and managed introduction of change, while fostering innovation. Key IT policies will be encoded in the digitized platform to allow business leaders at all levels to safely fulfill their day-to-day IT needs on their own. They will have the capabilities to manage projects and change, perform business process and information analysis, use configuration tools (to change processes, business rules, and information displayed, captured, analyzed, and reported), and troubleshoot systems issues.

Creating good IT is an important step, but it is simply the means to the end of having business leaders and professionals take direct control over the management of their IT assets. Business leaders have always wanted more direct control over information technology, as evidenced by their willingness to create shadow IT organizations, select technologies without involving IT, and contract directly with vendors. Business leaders *should have* more IT authority and responsibility. They run the business and should have control over all the key factors of production: money, people, and technology.

To support business IT self-sufficiency, a new IT organizational model and enabling technology will evolve that will allow IT to make sure IT is done well without trying to do it all. Trying to do it all on behalf of business partners results in tactically focused IT organizations that are too busy managing transactions to rise above the fray. Businesses need their IT organizations to help drive the definition of the company's operating model and supporting IT policies and architect a digitized business platform that enables and propagates innovations and reduces complexity and lights-on costs.

Giving business partners fish, rather than teaching them how to fish, not only slows the process and keeps IT in the weeds but also hinders the development of business leader IT smarts and alleviates their sense of responsibility for IT. In delegation lingo, it's called taking on someone else's monkey. It's impossible for IT to take care of everyone's monkey. Technology is evolving to a point, in terms of capability and criticality, that it makes sense for business leaders to share the job.

In democratizing innovation, IT will shift:

- **From direct to indirect control:** Instead of feeling compelled to be involved in every IT-related activity, IT will work with senior executives to define decision rights with assurance that leaders at every level will be held accountable for protecting enterprise interests.

- **From servicing to coaching:** Instead of trying to be a one-stop shop, IT will work with its business partners to increase their knowledge of systems, business processes, and information, assist in innovation and experimentation, and identify, justify, and deliver IT-enabled change.

- **From providing point solutions to providing enabling tools:** When properly architected and deployed, the combined effect of the emerging technologies discussed in chapter 7 and appendix B will be an industrial-strength innovators' toolkit that consists of Lego-like technology. These blocks will be in the hands of IT-smart, business leader digital natives, allowing them to fulfill their day-to-day IT needs on their own. Enterprise interests will be protected by the use of tools and automated processes that ensure integration, compliance, and operational performance.

- **From managing fixed assets to managing variable, on demand services:** With much of the IT activities distributed throughout the enterprise, flexible capacity will be essential. IT will deliver on demand, pay-per-use access to cost-effective computing, storage, and communications capacity.

Realistically, most organizations are far from possessing the capabilities necessary to responsibly democratize innovation. This goal won't be attained overnight. It will take the next decade or two. You can help accelerate the transformation by doing the following:

- *Assuming control* over the IT assets that fuel your business by creating a new partnership with IT.

- *Making IT self-sufficiency* a goal of every decision you make: in developing your organization, improving the relationship with IT, making strategy, sponsoring investments, defining functional requirements, determining service levels, and innovating.

- *Challenging the powers that be* to adopt "tight but loose" decision rights by defining boundary rules to delegate decision making to streamline governance and promote innovation.[5] IT boundary rules should guide behaviors that impact strategic priorities ("all new investments must benefit the customer"), investment levels ("IT funding will not negatively impact company margins"), architecture ("we will clean up as we go"), resource utilization ("we will maintain less than a 1:1 relationship between projects and people"), business value ("success will be gauged by measuring business impact and adoption"), risk ("every development initiative will improve our risk position"), and sourcing ("the best work will be done by our employees").

Democratizing innovation addresses IT's time-to-market issue, aligns accountability and responsibility for IT-enabled change, and unleashes innovation to exploit the marketplace opportunities inherent in the "connect and collaborate" future.[6] Pleasing business partners is not IT's ultimate goal. Rather, IT's ultimate goal is to ensure the success of the business. Help IT serve you *and* the business by making sure that IT isn't doing anything for you that you can, and should, do for yourself.

What's Next?

No rational person hates the people within IT, but everybody, IT and business leaders alike, hate the current IT system. Don't sit by and let IT become a strategic liability and the people within IT become increasingly marginalized, disrespected, and disengaged. If you think this statement is overly dramatic, check out some of the responses to the original "8 Things We Hate About IT" blog:

"These problems, combined with the lack of any sort of cohesive career path for programmers, are why I'm looking to get out of IT and I'm willing to take a substantial pay cut to do so."

"I worked in IT for fourteen years, and I left mainly due to the lack of respect and the fact I was tired of dealing with idiots."

"I am in IT and I wish I weren't."

Our companies can no longer afford to waste precious financial and human resources on IT "investments" that are sponsored by business leaders who believe IT is not their job and delivered by IT professionals who wish they weren't. To help position your company to realize the potential of great IT and fully democratized innovation, commit to creating a new partnership with IT.

Our individual, seemingly small actions create the building blocks of tomorrow. Leaders at all levels have a profound responsibility to leave their companies a little better than they found them. Achieving this goal requires personal integrity and the courage to think deeply about the ramifications of your actions, leading change before others ask or expect it. Don't complain about IT. Instead, do what you can, from where you are, to move past the frustrations and form a new partnership with IT.

Step up. Don't wait for IT to make the first move. Don't try to figure it all out in advance. In the words of John M. Richardson Jr., "When it comes to the future, there are three kinds of people: those who let it happen, those who make it happen, and those who wonder what happened."

Which one are you?

A Primer on Fast-Cycle Development

Make sure that IT uses a fast-cycle, value-driven process for developing new software. There are two basic types of development processes (or methodologies): waterfall and iterative. The *waterfall* methodology assumes that requirements can be defined at the beginning of the project and will not change throughout the project. *Iterative* approaches, on the other hand, assume that requirements will evolve throughout the initiative. Iterative approaches are more suitable for use in a dynamic business environment.

Iterative methodologies define requirements and deliver functionality in multiple iterations, allowing for the ultimate users to get early access to some functionality and to define requirements using a learn-by-doing approach. Iterative methodologies "view the project as series of smaller projects," enabling the project team "to test assumptions and refine the product in small increments, each of which has a better chance of being completed successfully."[1]

Iterative methodologies consist of phases; table 5-2 (see chapter 5) includes the phases—inception, elaboration, construction, and transition—of an iterative methodology called the Unified Process. Each of these phases is repeated every iteration, cycling through until the project is deemed "done enough." Other iterative methodologies, such as agile and scrum, are intense, collaborative efforts that cycle through iterations in a few weeks.

Other terms that you may hear thrown around are prototypes and pilots. *Prototypes* of systems can be used in iterative methodologies to confirm requirements. Prototypes are thrown together quickly and need to be discarded, because they aren't functional or robust enough to be deployed. *Pilots*, on the other hand, are limited implementations of iterations that will be modified by future iterations based on the results of the pilot.

To deliver capability every three to six months, something needs to be implemented that delivers value to the business—changes to people, processes, and technologies (or a subset of the three). Often, it's wise to test changes to the first two, leveraging existing systems with manual workarounds, before you develop or modify supporting technology.

Business leaders sometimes resist iterative development, because they've seen IT complete an iteration and then go off to greener project pastures because of a change in priorities. If you're using value-driven development and proving value realization along the way, you won't have a problem keeping everybody's attention, provided that the incremental return is attractive.

A methodology should be considered a guideline and not a hard-and-fast rule. Methodologies are useful in the hands of experienced IT professionals, and almost useless otherwise. As always, people are the key to success. Get the best people, make sure they sit together, and add value by making the work challenging, treating them with respect, and demonstrating trust by focusing on what needs to be accomplished, letting them determine how.

APPENDIX B

Emerging Technologies

The next wave of technology-enabled business impact will come from the power of quickly connecting companies, processes, people, computers, and physical devices to collaborate in new ways. Just thinking about the impact of powerful personal devices, low-cost sensors, ubiquitous high-capacity networks, vast quantities of data, and the broad array of interoperable technology services—all connected to the Internet—can make your head hurt. According to Eric Schmidt, CEO of Google,

> Everything will happen much faster . . . every product cycle, every information cycle, every bubble, will happen faster, because of network effects, where everybody is connected and talking to each other . . . The Internet levels playing fields in many ways—distribution, branding, money, and access . . . [and has] implications for the way corporations operate. They can't be as controlling. They have to let information out. They have to listen to their customers.[1]

Schmidt adds that "corporations will change the way they sell products to people who are increasingly computer assisted" and change the way they operate internally because the "wisdom of crowds argument is that you can operate a company by consensus."[2]

This "connect and collaborate" wave is also being fueled by dramatic improvements in the price performance of consumer technologies (semiconductors, network usage, communications bandwidth, and storage) as well as the emergence a new type of user—the *digital native*—who is comfortable using new technology and collaborating across time and space with people they have never met face-to-face or even conversed with over the phone.

Most of the technologies necessary to fuel the new business models in the "connect and collaborate" future already exist. The challenge for leaders is to architect a digitized platform that supports the business operating model and exploits the capabilities of the technologies without overdue complexity and costs.

Of course, "technology alone is rarely the key to unlocking economic value: companies create real wealth when they combine technology with new ways of doing business."[3] No one really knows where and how wealth will be created (and lost), but some very smart people are analyzing the moves of leading companies and making educated guesses:[4]

- **Distributed cocreation:** "Technology now allows companies to delegate substantial control to outsiders—cocreation— in essence by outsourcing innovation to business partners that work together in networks."

- **Using consumers as innovators:** "Companies that involve customers in design, testing, marketing, and the after-sales process get better insights into consumer needs and behavior and may be able to cut the cost of acquiring customers, engender greater loyalty, and speed up development cycles."

- **Tapping in to a world of talent:** "Software and internet technologies are making it easier and less costly for companies to integrate and manage the work of an expanding number of outsiders."

- **Extracting more value from interactions:** "Technology tools that promote tacit interactions, such as wikis, virtual team environments, and videoconferencing" are increasing the productivity of knowledge workers.

- **Expanding the frontiers of automation:** "Automate many repetitive tasks that aren't yet mediated by computers" [and] "interlink 'islands of automation' and so give managers and customers the ability to do new things."

- **Putting more science into management:** "Technology is helping managers exploit ever-greater amounts of data to make smarter decisions."

- **Unbundling production from delivery:** Companies can leverage investments in fixed costs by sharing these with other companies. For example, Amazon.com "has expanded its business model to let other retailers use its logistics and distribution services" and let others "buy processing power on its IT infrastructure."

- **Making business from information:** The vast amount of data across internal and external sources creates the "raw material for new information-based business opportunities."

To compete in this fast-paced, connected world, companies are changing the way they architect and build technology. According to Randy Heffner, a vice president at Forrester Research, "In this new world, it's not design the business and then design the technology, you're creating one thing, which is your business as embodied in your technology base."[5]

Companies will, over time, develop a digitized platform consisting of tools that help accelerate the deployment of new IT-enabled capabilities by empowering their workforce; reusing existing applications, information, and infrastructure services; connecting people and things together; and provisioning "on demand" technology capacity. Key technologies include:

- **Business process management** (BPM) software that allows for user-driven automation of manual tasks, including business process analysis, strategy, design, deployment, execution, operations, analysis, and optimization

- **Services-oriented architecture** (SOA) software that allows for the implementation of modular business processes using a modular approach to designing and developing software

- **Composite applications development** software that allows for the creation of user-driven applications from existing Web services, opening up new "possibilities for a new class of more short-term or disposable applications that could never meet the criteria for corporate investment"[6]

- **Master data management** software that allows for the delivery of consistent and accurate data (structured and unstructured) to all participants in the organizational ecosystem

- The **internet of people** that enables personalized, independent access to "software tools, information sources and social networks via the Web to support their jobs"[7]

- The **internet of things** that allows for business processes to be connected to and interact with physical objects. "If all cans, books, shoes or parts of cars are equipped with minuscule identifying devices, daily life on our planet will undergo a transformation. Things like running out of stock or wasted products will no longer exist as we will know exactly what is being consumed on the other side of the globe. Theft will be a thing of the past as we will know where a product is at all times. The same applies to parcels lost in the post."[8]

- **Unified communications** that integrates human communication and collaboration into business processes by embedding multiple styles and approaches (e.g., text, voice, video, etc.) into any application or interaction

- **Virtual IT infrastructure** that allocates resources when and where they are needed. This encompasses internal and external infrastructure and will result in dramatic increases in response time and IT operational productivity.

These technologies are essential to and will accelerate the democratization of IT as they support the movement "away from the practice of writing the business plan and then designing systems to support it" and facilitate the concurrent "design [of the] business and the systems that embody it."[9]

Key Responsibilities of the New Business– IT Partnership

- Service and control

  - **Business leaders:** Embrace enterprise interests, assume permanent responsibility for managing the IT assets that fuel your business, and work with IT as a partner rather than a customer.

  - **IT leaders:** Establish IT governance boards to clarify and streamline IT-related decision making, and create a business-savvy and service-oriented IT organization.

- Results and respect

  - **Business leaders:** Treat your IT relationship manager as a member of your team (and assign someone to fill the role if IT can't). Connect with the people in IT who facilitate the demand management process, support your business and systems, and manage and lead change. Do what you can to help ensure that the people you work with in IT feel challenged, respected, and connected.

— **IT leaders:** Hire professionals who are respected and collaborate well with the business, hold your people accountable for delivering on commitments, assign relationship managers to coordinate IT service delivery, and devote at least half of your time working outside IT with business partners.

- Tactics and strategies

    — **Business leaders:** Work with IT to understand, and derive if necessary, the IT-enabled business strategy for the enterprise, and develop the IT-enabled business strategy for your business unit.

    — **IT leaders:** Understand, and derive if necessary, the enterprise's business strategy, and facilitate the development of the IT-enabled business strategy (at the enterprise and business unit levels), including the definition of to-be and as-is architectures.

- Expense and investment

    — **Business leaders:** Obtain approval for IT-enabled business investments by navigating the demand management process, understand IT-related decision rights, and use operational measures to justify proposals, keep them on track, and validate value delivery.

- **IT leaders:** Ensure that IT governance is defined so that the business decides the "what" of IT and IT has authority over the "how" of IT. Help business partners navigate the demand management process and ensure that the mechanisms are in place to track value realized from IT-enabled investments.

- Quick and quality

  - **Business leaders:** Define a crystal-clear purpose for IT-enabled initiatives, and develop an approach that delivers value early and often. Assign top subject matter experts, foster constructive team dialogue, promote adoption of IT products by managing people and process change, help IT leverage existing technologies, and optimize end-to-end business processes.

  - **IT leaders:** Source top-quality project management, business analysis, engineering, and architectural talent, and establish flexible resourcing (human and technology) so that once a project is approved, it can be initiated in a timely fashion. Ensure that IT designs help move the organization toward target to-be architectures, and create project and change management processes that support fast-cycle delivery.

- Customization and standardization

  - **Business leaders:** Focus customization on necessary differences and understand and participate in the management of IT-related business risks. Increase technology adoption and exploitation, help ensure adequate KTLO funding, and support IT's cost reduction efforts.

— **IT leaders:** Define service catalogs and management processes to help business partners understand and request IT products and services. Provide consistent, predictable delivery, drive down year-over-year KTLO expenses, and define target architectures and infrastructure renewal plans.

- Innovation and bureaucracy

  — **Business leaders:** Invest in developing IT smarts, and lead by example through personal use and mastery of existing tools and systems. Elevate the relationship with IT leaders to free up their time to support lead user innovation. Actively manage the IT asset—and IT relationship—by holding your team accountable for exploiting the current technologies, innovating through experimentation, and understanding how to navigate the IT bureaucracy.

  — **IT leaders:** Ensure that the enhancement portion of the IT portfolio is managed by business unit investment boards. Build functionality that promotes business self-sufficiency, create an IT gifted-and-talented program that gives lead users special IT privileges, and support innovation through experimentation. Educate business partners on installed technologies and technology trends.

NOTES

Introduction

1. Susan Cramm, "8 Things We Hate About IT," Having IT Your Way blog, posted June 28, 2008, http://blogs.harvardbusiness.org/hbr/cramm/2008/06/8-things-we-hate-about-it.html.

2. Nicholas Carr, "IT Doesn't Matter," *Harvard Business Review*, May 2003, 41–49.

3. Ibid.

4. Susan Cramm, "How IT Smart Are Our Organizations?" Having IT Your Way blog, survey taken April–June 2009, with assistance from harvardbusiness.org.

5. To learn more, read Peter Weill and Jeanne Ross, *IT Savvy: What Top Executives Must Know to Go from Pain to Gain* (Boston: Harvard Business Press, 2009).

6. Cramm, "How IT Smart Are Our Organizations?"

7. Richard Nolan and F. Warren McFarlan, "Information Technology and the Board of Directors," *Harvard Business Review*, October 2005, 96–106.

8. http://www.quotedb.com/quotes/1360.

Chapter 1

1. To understand more about the people who gravitate to the technology profession, see the classic book by Paul Glen, David H. Maister, and Warren G. Bennis, *Leading Geeks: How to Manage and Lead the People Who Deliver Technology* (San Francisco: Jossey-Bass, 2003).

2. IT governance defines who makes IT-related decisions and how. There are five primary areas of IT governance: demand management, project management, service management, risk management, and architecture management.

3. "IT and Business Alignment Remains CIO's Top Concern," *Information Week*, September 3, 2008.

4. David Shpilberg, Steve Berez, Rudy Puryear, and Sachin Shah, "Avoiding the Alignment Trap in IT," *MIT Sloan Management Review*, Fall 2007, 51–58.

5. Peter Weill and Jeanne Ross, *IT Savvy: What Top Executives Must Know to Go from Pain to Gain* (Boston: Harvard Business Press, 2009).

6. Nicholas Carr, "IT Doesn't Matter," *Harvard Business Review*, May 2003, 41–49; and Susan Cramm, "How IT Smart Are Our Organizations?" Having IT Your Way Blog, survey taken April–June 2009, with assistance from harvardbusiness.org.

7. This number represents an average between two research studies evaluating the success of IT-enabled projects. Chris Sauer, Andrew Gemino, and Blaize Horner Reich, "Understanding Technology Project Risks and Predicting Project Performance," PowerPoint presentation, IS SIG Meeting, April 8, 2008, www.pmi.bc.ca/LinkClick.aspx?fileticket=YOhojYseIGM% 3D&tabid=224&mid=1562; and Standish Group, press release, April 23, 2009, http://www1.standishgroup.com/newsroom/chaos_2009.php.

8. Weill and Ross, *IT Savvy: What Top Executives Must Know to Go from Pain to Gain*, 11.

9. Ibid., 12.

10. George Westerman, "IT Risk Management: From IT Necessity to Strategic Business Value," working paper 366 (Cambridge, MA: Center for Information Systems Research, Sloan School of Management, MIT, December 2006), http://web.mit.edu/cisr/working%20papers/cisrwp366.pdf.

11. Forrester Research, *Q3 2008 Business Executive Survey*.

12. The Balanced Scorecard is a strategic planning and management system that is used to align business activities to the vision and strategy of the organization, improve internal and external communication, and monitor organization performance against strategic goals. For more information, see www.balancedscorecard.org.

13. Response to Susan Cramm, "8 Things We Hate About IT," Having IT Your Way Blog, posted June 28, 2008, http://blogs.harvardbusiness.org/hbr/cramm/2008/06/8-things-we-hate-about-it.html.

14. Gary Hamel, "CIOs Seen as Obstacles to Innovation," *CIO Insight,* September 13, 2007, http://www.cioinsight.com/c/a/Expert-Voices/CIOs-Seen-as-Obstacles-to-Innovation/.

15. *Jerry Maguire*, TriStar Pictures, 1996; directed by Cameron Crowe, written by Cameron Crowe.

Chapter 2

1. Paul Glen, David H. Maister, and Warren G. Bennis, *Leading Geeks: How to Manage and Lead the People Who Deliver Technology* (San Francisco: Jossey-Bass, 2003), 11, 39, and 42.

2. Responses to Susan Cramm, "8 Things We Hate About IT," Having IT Your Way blog, posted June 28, 2008, http://blogs.harvardbusiness.org/hbr/cramm/2008/06/8-things-we-hate-about-it.html.

3. Glen, Maister, and Bennis, *Leading Geeks: How to Manage and Lead the People Who Deliver Technology*, 21, 31, and 42.

4. Responses to Cramm, "8 Things We Hate About IT" blog.

5. This is a typical IT organization structure. Without a doubt, your IT organization will vary in how it groups and names the work, but rest assured, the work stays the same, whether some or all of it is done in-house or outsourced, decentralized, or centralized.

6. Averages based on a sampling of Valuedance clients.

7. Relationship managers are typically found in the application development group. They may or may not have staff reporting to them. If they do, they will focus primarily on application projects. More sophisticated IT organizations have expanded the relationship manager role to facilitate not only application services but also infrastructure services.

8. Glen, Maister, and Bennis, *Leading Geeks: How to Manage and Lead the People Who Deliver Technology*, 5.

9. Responses to Cramm, "8 Things We Hate About IT" blog.

10. Ibid.

11. Ibid.

Chapter 3

1. Susan Cramm, "How IT Smart Are Our Organizations?" Having IT Your Way blog, survey taken April–June 2009, with assistance from harvardbusiness.org.

2. Renée Dye and Olivier Sibony, "How to Improve Strategic Planning," *McKinsey Quarterly*, August 2007, 1.

Notes

3. For more, read Sarah Kaplan and Eric D. Beinhocker, "The Real Value of Strategic Planning," *MIT Sloan Management Review*, Winter 2003, 71–76.

4. Dan P. Lovallo and Lenny T. Mendonca, "Strategy's Strategist: An Interview with Richard Rumelt," *McKinsey Quarterly*, November 2007.

5. Process adapted from Marianne Broadbent and Ellen S. Kitzis, *The New CIO Leader: Setting the Agenda and Delivering Results* (Boston: Harvard Business School Press, 2004), chapters 2–4.

6. Process adapted from Clayton M. Christensen, "Making Strategy: Learning by Doing, *Harvard Business Review*, November–December 1997, 141–156.

7. Seth Kahan, "Lencioni Teaches Team Engagement," *Fast Company*, October 2009, http://www.fastcompany.com/blog/seth-kahan/leading-change/lencioni.

Chapter 4

1. Susan Cramm, "How IT Smart Are Our Organizations?" Having IT Your Way blog, survey taken April–June 2009, with assistance from harvard-business.org.

2. Ibid.

3. Although this approach makes life easier for the line manager, it results in a zillion "scratch my back" requests that overwhelm IT's supply and guarantees that IT will be primarily focused on tactics.

4. Nicholas Carr, "IT Doesn't Matter," *Harvard Business Review*, May 2003, 41–49.

5. Andrew McAfee, "The Case Against the Business Case," Andrew McAfee's blog, July 28, 2006, http://andrewmcafee.org/2006/07/the_case_against_the_business_case/.

6. Susan Cramm, "How IT Smart Are Our Organizations?"

7. Ibid.

8. Ibid.

9. David Mark and Eric Monnoyer, "Next Generation CIOs," *McKinsey on IT*, July 2004, 4.

10. Tom Davenport, "A Conversation With Peter Drucker," May 8, 2007, http://www.cio.com/article/108161/A_Conversation_With_Peter_Drucker?page=1, 6.

11. Ibid.

12. Jeff De Luca, "Requirements—The Budgeting Syndrome," *Feature Driven Development,* October 28, 2003, http://www.featuredrivendevelopment.com/node/614?PHPSESSID=32e8acdacdab3d89c51afd9c53019607.

Notes

13. Eric Monnoyer and Paul Willmott, "What IT Leaders Do," *McKinsey Quarterly*, August 2005, http://www.mckinseyquarterly.com/Information_Technology/What_IT_leaders_do_1652.

Chapter 5

1. These numbers represents an average between two research studies evaluating the success of IT-enabled projects. Chris Sauer, Andrew Gemino, and Blaize Horner Reich, "Understanding Technology Project Risks and Predicting Project Performance," PowerPoint presentation, IS SIG Meeting April 8, 2008, www.pmi.bc.ca/LinkClick.aspx?fileticket=YOhojYseIGM%3D&tabid=224&mid=1562; and Standish Group, press release April 23, 2009, http://www1.standishgroup.com/newsroom/chaos_2009.php.

2. Susan Cramm, "How IT Smart Are Our Organizations?" Having IT Your Way blog, survey taken April–June 2009, with assistance from harvardbusiness.org.

3. Paul Glen, David H. Maister, and Warren G. Bennis, *Leading Geeks: How to Manage and Lead the People Who Deliver Technology* (San Francisco: Jossey-Bass, 2003), 58.

4. Enterprise resource planning applications "can be used to manage product planning, parts purchasing, inventories, interacting with suppliers, providing customer service, and tracking orders. ERP can also include application modules for the finance and human resources aspects of a business"; http://searchsap.techtarget.com/sDefinition/0,,sid21_gci213946,00.html.

5. Jim Johnson, *My Life Is Failure: 100 Things You Should Know to Be a Better Project Leader* (Boston: Standish Group International, 2006), 160.

6. Susan Cramm, "IT Project Planning: Adult Supervision Required," *CIO Magazine*, March 2001: http://www.cio.com.au/article/33240/adult_supervision_required?fp=512&fpid=1376906222&rid=1.

7. John Thorpe, *Information Paradox* (New York: McGraw Hill, 2003), 38.

8. David Rock and Jeffrey Schwartz, "The Neuroscience of Leadership," *Strategy+Business,* November 2, 2006, http://www.strategy-business.com/webinars/webinar/webinar-neuro_lead.

9. Adapted from Ric Merrifield, Jack Calhoun, and Dennis Stevens, "The Next Revolution in Productivity," *Harvard Business Review*, June 2008, 72–80.

10. Jeanne W. Ross, Peter Weill, and David C. Robertson, *Enterprise Architecture as Strategy: Creating a Foundation for Business Execution* (Boston: Harvard Business School Publishing, 2006).

Notes

11. Watts S. Humphrey, "Why Big Software Projects Fail: The 12 Key Questions," *STSC Crosstalk,* March 2005, http://www.stsc.hill.af.mil/CrossTalk/2005/03/0503Humphrey.html.

12. Jeff De Luca, "Requirements—The Budgeting Syndrome," *Feature Driven Development*, October 28, 2003, http://www.featuredrivendevelopment.com/node/614?PHPSESSID=32e8acdacdab3d89c51afd9c53019607.

13. To learn more, see Sam Marwaha et al., "The Next Generation of In-House Software Development," *McKinsey Quarterly*, Spring 2006.

14. To learn more, see James M. Kaplan et al., "Managing Next-Generation IT Infrastructure," *McKinsey Quarterly,* February 2005.

15. Joseph Grenny, David Maxfield, and Andrew Shimberg, "How Project Leaders Can Overcome the Crisis of Silence," *MIT Sloan Management Review*, July 2007, 46–52.

16. David Mark and Eric Monnoyer, "Next Generation CIOs," *McKinsey on IT*, July 2004, 4.

Chapter 6

1. "The objective of Change Management in this context is to ensure that standardized methods and procedures are used for efficient and prompt handling of all changes to controlled IT infrastructure, in order to minimize the number and impact of any related incidents upon service," http://en.wikipedia.org/wiki/Change_Management_(ITSM).

2. "Service level" (definition), *PCMag.com Encyclopedia*, http://www.pcmag.com/encyclopedia_term/0,2542,t=service+level&i=51183,00.asp.

3. Nicholas Carr, "IT Doesn't Matter," *Harvard Business Review*, May 2003, 41–49.

4. Ibid.

5. Ibid.

6. Peter Weill and Jeanne W. Ross, *IT Savvy: What Top Executives Must Know to Go from Pain to Gain* (Boston: Harvard Business Press, 2009), 11.

7. Chad Dickerson, "The Top 20 IT Mistakes to Avoid," *InfoWorld,* www.infoworld.com/print/13314.

8. Anthony Sibillin, "Data Storage: No Room at the Inn," *CFO,* January 2, 2002, http://www.cfo.com/article.cfm/3002726?f=related.

9. John Bace, Carol Rozwell, Joseph Feiman, and Bill Kirwin, *Understanding the Costs of Compliance* (Stamford, CT: Gartner, 2006), http://logic.stanford.edu/POEM/externalpapers/understanding_the_costs_of_c_13 8098.pdf.

10. Weill and Ross, *IT Savvy*, 12.

11. Services should be defined in terms that business leaders can understand (such as SAP, facilities moves, mobile support, etc.). IT organizations far and wide are scurrying around defining services and developing service catalogs to help business leaders make responsible "buying" decisions and to facilitate effective service delivery. Identifying services is fundamental to effective service management so that business needs can be addressed in a cost-effective manner. Decomposing IT costs by business unit, technology product, and service, called *IT cost transparency*, requires applying activity-based costing disciplines, a capability typically not found in most companies.

12. From business leader phone interviews conducted by the author, March 2009.

13. Susan Cramm, "How IT Smart Are Our Organizations?" Having IT Your Way blog, survey taken April–June 2009, with assistance from harvard-business.org.

14. Dan Tynan, "16 Ways IT Can Do Less with Less," *InfoWorld*, March 16, 2009, www.infoworld.com/print/6799.

15. Alan McCarthy, "Implementing ITIL and Service Management," British Computer Society, November 2006, http://www.bcs.org/server.php?show=conWebDoc.8080.

16. Interviews with IT leaders conducted by author, May 2009.

17. Brenda Iniguez, "How ITIL Is Changing the Workplace: The New Generation Service Desk," presentation, HDI Capital Area Local Chapter, October 30, 2008.

18. John Soat, "HP CIO Randy Mott: Increment IT Just Doesn't Work," InformationWeek's CIO Uncensored Weblog, January 2008, http://www.informationweek.com/blog/main/archives/2008/01/hp_cio_randy_mo.html;jsessionid=YTWPLZHZU3ILBQE1GHOSKH4ATMY32JVN.

19. Alex Cullen, "The Business-IT Expectation Gap," Forrester Research, November 7, 2008.

20. Current regulations include, for example, the U.S. Sarbanes-Oxley Act, which requires companies to certify the accuracy and accountability of financial data; the Health Insurance Portability and Accountability Act; and the Gramm-Leach-Bliley Act, which require companies to protect confidential data.

21. Framework based on George Westerman, "Understanding the Enterprise's IT Risk Profile" (Boston: MIT Sloan Center for Information Systems Research, March 2004).

22. Karen Kotowski, Governance/Risk/Compliance panel, MIT CIO Conference, Boston, May 19, 2009.

Chapter 7

1. Innovation is about discovering new ways of attracting and keeping customers and is more important than ever, given the global nature of competition fueled by technologies that shift power to the customer; change the nature and process by which products and services are developed; reduce the costs of marketing, production, and distribution; and remove traditional company boundaries. In a 2008 McKinsey survey, almost "two-thirds of respondents say their organizations are at risk from information and technology-based disruption" because of "shifts in customer expectations for better products or differentiated services enabled by information- and technology-based capabilities" and "competitors using technology to significantly reduce the cost of manufacturing or delivering of current products or services," with less than half of the respondents feeling that "their companies are well prepared to meet these risks." Business Technology Office, "IT's Unmet Potential: McKinsey Global Survey Results," *McKinsey Quarterly*, December 2008, https://www.mckinseyquarterly.com/ghost.aspx?ID=/Telecommunications/ITs_unmet_potential_McKinsey_Global_Survey_Result_2277. Innovation can fall in a continuum from big (a new business model) to small (continuous improvement) or somewhere in between. Innovation is an experiential process, initially limited in scope and typically spearheaded by the passions and ingenuity of individuals and small teams from all levels.

2. Susan Cramm, "How IT Smart Are Our Organizations?" Having IT Your Way blog, survey taken April–June 2009, with assistance from harvardbusiness.org.

3. Chris Andersen, "Who Needs a CIO?" The Long Tail, posted February 27, 2007.

4. Peter Weill and Jeanne W. Ross, *IT Savvy: What Top Executives Must Know to Go from Pain to Gain* (Boston: Harvard Business Press, 2009), 74, 78.

5. To learn more, see ibid.

6. Eric Von Hippel, *Democratizing Innovation* (Cambridge, MA: The MIT Press, 2006).

7. Ibid., 1.

8. Joachim Ackermann et al., "Better IT Management for Banks," *McKinsey Quarterly*, July 2007.

Notes

9. Weill and Ross, *IT Savvy*, 14.
10. Cramm, "How IT Smart Are Our Organizations?"
11. Interviews by author, June 2009.
12. Von Hippel, *Democratizing Innovation*, 8.
13. Interviews by author, May 2009.
14. Interview by author, June 2009.
15. http://www.goodreads.com/quotes/show/683.
16. http://www.goodquotes.com/sillyquotes.htm.
17. Source unknown—heard by the author early in her career.
18. Cramm, "How IT Smart Are Our Organizations?"
19. Interviews by author, June 2009.
20. "Companies Use Only Two-Thirds of ERP System Functionality," *InfoWorld*, May 15, 2009, http://www.infoworld.com/print/75622.
21. Concept adapted from Von Hippel, *Democratizing Innovation*.
22. Interviews conducted by author, June 2009.
23. Interviews conducted by author, June 2009.

Chapter 8

1. Scott Keller, "The Irrational Side of Change Management," *McKinsey Quarterly*, Month TK 2009, 12.
2. Alignment framework adapted from Gartner as overviewed in "What Is IT's Role?", ITBusinessEdge, February 2006, http://www.itbusinessedge.com/topics/reader.aspx?oss=12679.
3. Roger Roberts and Tom Stephenson, "Managing IT to Support Rapid Growth: An Interview with the CIO of NetApp," *McKinsey Quarterly*, June 2008, http://www.mckinseyquarterly.com/managing_it_support_interview_with_CIO_of_NetApp_2154.
4. Ibid.
5. To learn more about boundary rules, read Kathleen M. Eisenhardt and Donald N. Sull, "Strategy as Simple Rules," *Harvard Business Review*, January 2001, 106–116.
6. To learn more about the future of IT, see Susan Cramm, "Circa 2015: The CIO of the Future," September 2008, available at www.valuedance.com.
7. http://www.businessweek.com/managing/content/jun2008/ca2008064_652958.htm; and http://blogs.harvardbusiness.org/hbr/cramm/2008/06/8-things-we-hate-about-it.html.

Notes

Appendix A

1. Paul Glen, David H. Maister, and Warren G. Bennis, *Leading Geeks: How to Manage and Lead the People Who Deliver Technology* (San Francisco: Jossey-Bass, 2003), 94.

Appendix B

1. Eric Schmidt, quoted in James Manyika, "Google's View of the Future of Business: An Interview with CEO Eric Schmidt," *McKinsey Quarterly*, September 2008.
2. Ibid.
3. James M. Manyika et al., "Eight Business Technology Trends to Watch," *McKinsey Quarterly*, December 2007.
4. Ibid.
5. Rich Seeley, "Forrester: Digital Business Architecture emerges from SOA," SearchSOA.com, May 2006, http://searchsoa.techtarget.com/news/article/0,289142,sid26_gci1188336,00.html.
6. "Four Disruptions That Will Transform the Software Industry," Thomas Wailgum, CIO.com, October 2008, http://www.cio.com/article/print/454930.
7. Eric Chabrow, "6 New Must-Know IT Trends," *Parallax View CIO Insight,* August 2008, http://blogs.cioinsight.com/parallax_view/content/emerging_technology/6_new_mustknow_it_trends.html.
8. Wikipedia, http://en.wikipedia.org/wiki/Internet_of_Things.
9. Ibid.

INDEX

accessibility, 121, 122
accountability, 152
  for configuration, 119
  decision rights and, 65, 68–71
  in demand management, 65–66
  democratizing innovation and, 155
  for innovation, 129–130
  for returns, 79
  for risk management, 120–123
  for strategy, 45–46, 57, 60
  user, 109
account managers. *See* relationship managers
accuracy, 121, 122
affordability of initiatives, 73
agility, 110, 121, 122, 145
airline industry, 50
alignment
  customization versus standardization and, 110–111
  of investments, 79
  IT–business, 22–24
  prioritization of, 25–26
  project approval and, 56–58
  relationship managers in promoting, 46

  for service and control, 17–18
  strategic versus tactics, 43–62
Amazon.com, 44, 163
American Airlines, 44
Apple, 31
application services, 33, 35, 36
approval of projects, 46–47
architecture, 49–54
  assessing, 145
  documentation of, 112–113
  emerging technologies in, 164
  enhancements to, 110
  great IT and, 153
  predefined, for quality and quickness, 100
  services-oriented, 164, 166
architecture management, 70
authority, 16–17, 25
automation, 117–118, 123, 163

Balanced Scorecard, 19, 77
Barker, Colin, 122
Bennis, Warren G., 31, 86–87
build-to-order approach, 100–101
bureaucracy, 31–32
  innovation versus, 125–127

bureaucracy (*continued*)
key responsibilities in, 172
in service versus control, 16–17
business analysts, 36
business cases, 77–78, 90–91, 133
cost reduction and, 118
business drivers
importance versus support of, 56
in strategic planning, 54–56
business intelligence (BI), 91
business process management
(BPM), 91, 164, 166
Business Technology Office, 122
"butler" view of IT, 147
buy-in
decision making and, 70–71
for results, 30–31
for strategy, 43–44, 58–62

Carr, Nicholas, 114
challenge
IT personnel desire for, 37–38, 41
change
accountability for, 129–130
assessing management of, 145
emergency system care and, 113
engaging others in, 92–93
IT as wet blanket in, 22–24
IT-enabled, difficulty of, 87–89
resistance to, 131
technology enhancements for, 110
change agents, 88–89
change management process,
108–109, 145
CIOs
IT organization and, 32–33
relationship management
and, 35, 36
in strategic alignment, 47–48

clean-as-you-go approach, 52, 53
cocreation, distributed, 162
collaboration, 21
democratizing innovation
and, 155
facilitating, 93
innovation and, 137
in investment decision making,
70–71
with IT, 150
Web 2.0, 166
web publishing and, 137
commitment, to investments, 73.
See also buy-in
communication
innovation and, 136
plan, 93
unified, 165, 167
complexity, 52–54, 126, 153
compliance, 108, 115
composite applications development, 164, 166
"concierge" view of IT, 147
configuration features, 119
configuration tools, 104
connect and collaborate, 155,
161–167
connections, personal, 39–40, 41. *See
also* relationship management
consolidation, 117, 126
construction phase of projects,
98, 157
consultants, 29–30, 61, 132–133
consumption, reducing, 117
context of use requirements, 136
control
direct versus indirect, 153
innovation and, 152
key responsibilities in, 169
versus service, 15–28

costs
  assessing management of, 146
  distribution of, 114–117
  of downtime, 111
  expenses versus investment,
    63–83
  as expenses versus investment,
    63–83, 170–171
  importance of IT, 114
  of initiatives, 73
  innovation and, 131–132
  keep the lights on (KTLO),
    67, 70, 71, 75, 115–119
  key responsibilities in, 170–171
  lights-on, 19, 21, 113, 114
  operational, 19
  outsourcing and, 128–129
  partnership for managing, 123
  reducing, 116–119
  regulatory compliance, 115
  uncertainty and, 132–133
Cramm, Susan, 45, 79
customer relationship management
    (CRM) systems, 76, 91
customers
  emerging technologies and,
    162
  innovation by, 162–163
  partners versus, 24–26
  perspective of in strategy
    development, 61
  understanding, 50–51
customization, 27, 108
  costs in, 114–117
  emergency care and, 111–113
  key responsibilities in, 171–172
  production and, 108–110
  risk management and, 119–123
  standardization versus,
    107–123

data management, master, 164, 166
data storage costs, 115
Dearborn, Rob, 111
decentralization, 25
decision making
  collaborative, 70–71
  IT professionals in, 39
  for project quality and quickness,
    101–103
  rights in, 65, 68–71, 154–155
  in service versus control, 16–17
  strategy as driver in, 44–45, 49, 59
demand management process,
    58, 63–83
  challenges in, 78–80
  as cyclical process, 66
  decision rights in, 65, 68–71
  definition of, 64
  financial planning in, 65, 71–72
  portfolio management in,
    65, 67–68
  prioritization in, 64, 65, 72–75
  for production, 110
  purpose of, 66–67
  worthwhile investments in,
    80–82
Dickerson, Chad, 122
digital natives, 162
distributed cocreation, 162
documentation, 108, 112–113
downtime, 111–113
Drucker, Peter, 80

economies of scale, 71
education
  for IT management, 25
  user, 109
efficiency, 19, 21
Einstein, Albert, 10

Index

elaboration phase of projects, 98, 157
emergency system care, 111–113
emerging technologies, 161–167
emotional involvement.
    See also buy-in
  getting results through, 30–31
  quality versus quickness
    and, 89
  in strategic planning, 58–62
enabling tools, 153–154
enhancement investments, 67–68, 79, 131–132, 172
  financial planning for, 71–72
enterprise architecture, 49–54
enterprise interests
  assessing, 145–146
  customer versus partner relationships in, 24–26
  federated model to balance, 34
  innovation and, 126–127
  line leader promotion of, 20–22
  reconciling competing, 19–20
enterprise operating model, 49–54
enterprise resource planning (ERP) software, 1, 87–89, 101–102
"entrepreneur" view of IT, 148
Excel, 136–137
experimentation, 132–135
Extended Internet, 166

fast-cycle development, 157–159.
    See also time frames
feature creep, 90
federated model, 34
feedback, 146–147
financial planning, 65, 71–72
flexibility, 110, 145

Forrester Research, 164
Frito-Lay, 44
frontline employees, equipping, 90–91
functionality
  cost reduction and, 118
  utilization of, 1, 97, 136
future, securing, 19, 21

Glen, Paul, 31, 86–87
goals. *See* objectives
good versus great, 8, 141–156, 127
governance structure, 171
  decision rights and, 70, 154–155
  innovation and, 150–151, 152
  IT, 32–34
  in service versus control, 16–17
"grinder" view of IT, 148, 149

Hamel, Gary, 22
Harvard Business Review, 2
Have IT Your Way, 9
Heffner, Randy, 164
Hewlett-Packard, 119
horizontal integration, 110
"How IT Smart Are Our Organizations?" (Cramm), 45
"How IT-Smart Are Our Organizations?" survey, 146

implementation
  iterative approach in, 10–11
  project-based, 57
inception phase of projects, 98, 157
incident reports, 109
Information Paradox (Thorpe), 89

Index

infrastructure, 48
off-the-shelf, 100–101
organic IT, 167
virtual, 165
infrastructure services, 33
issue resolution by, 109
relationship building with, 36
initiatives
affordability of, 73
assessing management of, 145
challenges facing, 78–80
commitment to, 73
experimentation versus, 132–135
kill switches for, 99
ranking, 73
risk management for, 73
risk of, 73
in strategic planning, 54–56
as strategy, 46–47
value of, 72, 73
innovation, 18
accountability for, 129–130
in architecture reusing stage, 53
assessing management of, 146
bureaucracy versus, 125–140
complexity and, 126
consumers in, 162–163
democratizing, 150–152, 153–155
enterprise interests and, 126–127
experimentation in, 132–135
fostering, 27
governance and, 150–151
IT as wet blanket in, 22–24,
125–126
IT-smart, 135–138
IT's reputation for, 22–24
key responsibilities in, 172
maintenance versus, 50–51
outsourcing and, 128–129

partnership for, 138–140
relationship management and,
130–132
resources for, 127–128
technology in, 138
toolkits for, 136–137
uncertainty in, 132–133
internet of people, 165
internet of things, 165
investments, 27. See also demand
management process
accountability for, 70–71
boards, project approval by, 46–47
demand management process
for, 58
enhancement, 67–68, 71–72
experiment approach to, 132–135
financial planning for, 65, 71–72
funding for, 77–78
in IT smarts, 135–138
key responsibilities in, 170–171
partnership for, 82–83
prioritizing, 64, 65, 72–75
returns on, 63–83
strategic, 68, 72
value management for, 75–77
worthwhile, 80–82
IT
architecture maintenance, 49–54
assessment of current, 48
attempts to bypass, 29–30
blaming the system versus the
people in, 3–6
business leader knowledge
about, 22–24
capital spending on, 75
causes of bad, 148–150
characteristics of people in,
16, 30–32, 37–40

IT (*continued*)
    as competitive weapon, 19, 114
    as core competence, 9–10
    criticism of, 2–3
    current versus new, 95–96
    deserved capability of, 147–148
    desire for connection in, 39–40
    desire for respect in, 38–39
    desire to be challenged in, 37–38, 41
    desire to please in, 15–16
    emergency care in, 111–113
    future of, 155–156
    good versus great, 8, 27, 141–156
    governance of, 32–34, 70
    great, 152–155
    involving in project development, 75
    key responsibilities in, 169–172
    limits of, 150–152
    management, assessing, 142–147
    motivation of, 37–40
    organization of, 32–34
    outsourcing, 128–129
    plans for, 48
    self-sufficiency of, 152–153, 154
    shadow organizations in, 103–104
    strategy of, 48
    views of, 148
IT business office, 32–33
"IT Doesn't Matter," (Carr) 2
iterative approach, 10–11, 157–159
IT investment boards, 71–72
IT Savvy (Weill and Ross), 6

Kantor, Rosabeth Moss, 53
Kaplan, Robert S., 19
"keep the lights on" (KTLO)
    expenses, 67, 70, 75, 115–116
    planning for, 71

    reducing, 116–119
    risk management and, 121, 123
kill switches, 99
Kotowski, Karen, 123

layer and leave approach, 51
leadership
    accountability in, 129–130
    bad IT and, 149–150
    as customers versus partners, 24–26
    decision rights and, 65, 68–71
    developing IT-smart, 6–8
    enterprise interest promotion by, 20–22
    IT, partnership with, 26
    IT knowledge of, 22–24
    IT-smart, 103–104
    key responsibilities in, 169–172
    for quality and quickness, 99
    relationship management with, 36
    in risk management, 120–123
    in strategy, 45–46
Leading Geeks (Glen, Maister, and Bennis), 31
lead users, 127–128, 130, 137–138
learning
    documenting, 142
    by doing, 97
    from experiments, 134
    stages in, 52–53
leveraging
    existing technology, 95–96
    in investments, 80
lights-on costs, 19, 113
    assessing management of, 146
    efficiency in, 21
localizing stage of architecture, 52–53

maintenance, 49–54, 110
Maister, David H., 31, 86–87
management. *See also* relationship
    managers
    of change, 36
    emerging technologies in, 163
    IT leader relationships with,
        30–31
    in quickness versus quality, 86
    of technology versus being
        managed by, 3
mashups, Web, 164, 166
master data management, 164,
    166
McAfee, Andrew, 76
McCartney, Scott, 50
McKinsey Quarterly, 82
mental models, negative, 5–6
metrics
    core operating, 110
    for driving forces, 57
    for project quality, 97
    for returns, 75–77
    service levels, 108
Microsoft, 30–31
Microsoft Word, 1
modernization, 117
Monnoyer, Eric, 82
motivation, 37–40, 91–92
Mott, Randy, 119

NetApp, 150–151
Norton, David P., 19

objectives
    clarity in, 86, 88
    for driving forces, 57
    involving IT in setting, 38, 39

in IT-enabled business strategy, 55
    progress toward, 74
    risk management and, 88
operational costs, 19
operational support view of IT, 148
optimizing stage of architecture,
    52, 53
outsourcing, 29–30, 34, 128–129

partnerships
    business leaders in, 24–26
    for cost management, 123
    with external IT providers, 150
    for great IT, 153
    for innovation, 138–140
    for investments, 82–83
    key responsibilities in, 169–172
    new IT, 27–28
    perspective of in strategy
        development, 61
    for quality and quickness,
        104–105
    for results and respect, 40–41
    for tactics and strategy, 62–63
performance
    brainstorming about, 55
    effective technology deployment
        and, 18
    process optimization and, 94–95
pervasive interactions, 166
pilot projects, 81–82, 134–135, 157
planning
    errors in, 58–62
    facts in, 102
    financial, 65, 71–72
    IT organization and, 32–33
    relationship management and, 36
portfolio management, 65, 67–68,
    172

Index

portfolio managers. *See* relationship managers

power, costs of, 115

prioritization

in demand management, 64, 65, 72–75

investment, 81–82

of process improvement, 94

privacy issues, 120

processes

cost reduction and, 117

documentation of, 112–113

identifying critical, 94

integrating and streamlining, 89

optimizing, 93–95

people behind, 31–32

in quality and quickness, 93–95

responding to opportunities in, 50–51

in risk management, 123

understanding IT, 7

production, 107–108, 163

productivity tools, 136–137, 163

program management office, 32–33

project approval, 46–47, 102

demonstrating alignment for, 56–58

elevator pitch for, 57

project management, 70

project managers, 36

project teams, 4, 100, 101–102, 108

prototypes, 134–135, 157

purchases

delaying, 117

quality versus cost in, 118–119

quality, 36

communication for, 101–103

of current versus new technology, 95–96

difficulty of in IT-enabled change, 87–89

engaging others in, 92–93

involving IT in, 103–104

key responsibilities in, 171

partnership for, 104–105

processes and, 93–95

project size and, 96–101

purpose definition and, 89, 90–92

quickness versus, 85–105

regulation, 108, 115, 120

relationship management, 27

attempts to bypass IT in, 29–30

connections in, 39–40

in decision making, 49

as end rather than means, 40

importance of, 7–8

innovation and, 130–132

key responsibilities in, 169–170

negative mental models and, 5–6

resistance to, 131

for results and respect, 34–37

relationship managers, 25, 34–37

in financial planning, 72

respecting, 41

in risk management, 120–121

in strategic alignment, 46, 47–48

as team members, 136

requirements, defining, 86, 130

resource management, 64. *See also* demand management process

for innovation, 127–128

respect versus results, 29–41

responsibility. *See* accountability

Index

results versus respect, 29–41
  IT organization and, 32–34
  key responsibilities in, 169–170
  new partnership for, 40–41
  people behind, 31–32
  relationship management in,
    34–37
  understanding IT personnel and,
    37–40
returns, 63–83
  average, 76
  metrics for, 75–77
  partnership for, 82–83
  value management for, 75–77
reusing stage of architecture, 52, 53
risk management, 119–123
  evaluating technology and, 113
  honesty in assessment for, 102
  in investment prioritization, 73
  investments and, 68
  IT costs and, 114
  iterative approach and, 10–11
  in IT governance, 70
  objective definition and, 88
  objectives in, 121, 122
  in projects, 102–103
road maps, implementation, 57
Robertson, David C., 52–53
Ross, Jeanne, 6, 52–53
Rumelt, Richard, 46

Sallie Mae, 123
Schmidt, Eric, 161–162
scrap and rebuild, 51
security, 120
self-help diagnostics, 104
service catalogs, 25, 172
service levels, 108, 119

service management, 70, 154
services-oriented architecture
  (SOA), 164, 166
service versus control, 15–28
  alignment for both, 17–20
  business leaders as customers or
    partners and, 24–26
  IT knowledge and, 22–24
  key responsibilities in, 169
simplification, 52–54
social networking, 166
solutions versus enabling tools,
  153–154
spreadsheets, 136–137
stakeholders, 16
  elevator pitch for, 57
  initiative funding and, 78
standardization, 27
  complexity and, 126
  costs in, 114–117
  customization versus, 107–123
  emergency care and, 111–113
  key responsibilities in, 171–172
  risk managemant and, 119–123
  stage of architecture, 52, 53
strategic alignment versus tactics,
  43–62
  key responsibilities in, 170
strategic investments, 68, 72
strategy
  accountability for, 45–46, 57
  alignment with, 17–18
  buy-in with, 43–44, 58–62
  as decision driver, 44–45
  decision rights and, 154–155
  definition of, 43
  delegating responsibility for, 61
  demand management and,
    64–65

strategy (*continued*)
enterprise operating model and, 49–54
importance of, 44–45
IT-enabled, 46–47
components of, 48
deriving, 54–56
determining existence of, 47–54
quality and, 104
logic in, 62
making, strategic thinking versus, 61
planning versus doing, 62
as process versus event, 60–61
project approval and alignment with, 46–47, 56–58
purpose and, 92
value realization and, 18
writing down, 46–47
strategy matrix, 57
support. *See also* buy-in
for current operations, 74
innovation and, 130–132
for projects, 88, 102
SWOT (strengths, weaknesses, opportunities, and threats) analysis, 56

tactics versus strategic alignment, 43–62
talent
assigning to investments, 80
emerging technologies and, 163
for project teams, 100
for quality, 105
supporting, 130
"team player" view of IT, 148
teams

emergency care, 112–113
project, 4, 100, 101–102, 108
relationship managers in, 136
strategic planning, 54
technology
emerging, 161–167
in innovation, 138
leveraging existing, 95–96
risk management and, 113
testing, 98, 108
Thorpe, John, 89
time frames
for change, 10–11
conversations for enabling, 101–103
for delivery, 27, 34
democratizing innovation and, 155
emerging technologies and, 161–162
fast-cycle development, 157–159
IT challenges in, 97–99
key responsibilities in, 171
partnership for, 104–105
processes and, 93–95
for project implementation, 58
project size and, 96–101
purpose definition and, 89, 90–92
quality versus, 85–105
short versus long, 86, 89, 96
to-be enterprise architecture, 54
transition phase of projects, 98, 157
troubleshooting, 109, 111–113
Tynan, Dan, 121, 122

UC platforms, 167
uncertainty, 132–133

Index

Unified Process, 157
users
  educating, 109
  lead, 127–128
  support programs for, 130
utilization, 1, 97, 117, 136

value, 11
  assessing management of, 145
  in demand management,
    65–66
  development driven by, 157
  extracting from interactions, 163
  of initiatives, 72, 73, 79
  in investment prioritization, 72
  managing, 75–77
  outsourcing and, 128–129

  realizing, 18, 21
  of strategic planning, 44–45
vendors, 29–30
virtual infrastructure, 165
Von Hippel, Eric, 129–130

Walmart, 44
waterfall methodology, 157
Web 2.0, 166
Web mashups, 164, 166
Weill, Peter, 6, 52–53
wikis, 163
Willmott, Paul, 82
Winnie the Pooh, 128

X Internet, 166

ABOUT THE AUTHOR

Susan Cramm is an executive coach and president of Value-dance, an executive coaching and leadership development firm specializing in information technology. A recognized industry expert, she helped pioneer the field of IT leadership coaching through her passion and gifts for developing others, as well as her keen, practical insights derived from extensive research and years of coaching and serving in executive-level positions. Over the past twelve years, Susan has worked with executives from a number of *Fortune* 500 clients, including Toyota, Sony, and Whole Foods Markets, and her clients describe her as insightful, motivational, practical, tough, committed, and invaluable. She is a frequent speaker at industry conferences, a prolific writer, and author of the *Harvard Business Review* blog "Have IT Your Way."

Susan is the former Chief Financial Officer and executive vice president at Chevy's Mexican Restaurants, where she led the finance, business strategy, restaurant development, franchising, legal, and information technology functions. Prior to Chevy's, she worked with Taco Bell Corporation and held the positions of Chief Information Officer and vice president of the Information Technology Group and senior director for financial and strategic planning.

About the Author

Susan received her master's degree in management from Northwestern University, specializing in finance, marketing, and quantitative methods, and her BA from University of California, San Diego, summa cum laude, specializing in management and computer science. She lives in San Clemente, California, with her husband, Bryan; daughter, Jessica; dog, Jasmine; and grumpy old cat, Yote.